Here We Go Joe

How one family created a final home for a father with dementia with love, honor, and dignity.

Here We Go Joe Printed in the United States by Createspace

Edited and designed by The Cheerful Word LLC

Cover and book design by Meghan McDonald

Cover art by Hannah Darrah

Bible references:
Holy Bible
New International Version, June 1978
(Revised August 1983)
The Committee on Bible Translation
Names of the translators and editors may be secured from the International Bible Society, translation sponsors of the New International Version, 144 Tices Lane, East Brunswick, New Jersey 08816

ISBN: 13:9781515023180

First printing, 2015

Additional copies can be ordered through www.amazon.com

The Cheerful Word LLC
www.CheerfulWord.com

Dedication

This book is dedicated to my husband Jay,
his sister Mary Beth, and their father Joe.
For allowing me into a family filled with
cherished memories.

Table of Contents

Testimonials

From a Marketing Director point of view, my job is to try to help families with one of the most difficult, gut wrenching decisions of placing mom or dad in assisted living. Every day, I walk and talk and hug with residents, I feel like I make a difference in their lives providing an ear to a story, a shoulder for a lonely day, or just a good ole fashion hug. BUT, after reading *Here We Go Joe*, it opened my eyes to see that each resident has their own stories, trials, and tribulations. I thank Cora not only for opening my eyes, but for her insight and compassion in sharing Joe's journey and reminding us all to look beyond the obvious.

Lin Schultz
Marketing Director
Croatan Village

Hi, I just finished reading your book. I liked the verses before each chapter. Very well done. It brought back so many Joe memories...His stubbornness especially. But, I had to smile several times. A perfect picture of his personality. I remember all the cleaning you did.....a good laugh with some sadness of course.

Sue Bowersock
Occupational Therapist and Joe's former neighbor

Cora, your book is such a beautiful thing. You not only have taken care of my brother, but I have also found some of myself in him with some of the things he has told you and others. I can understand a lot of his attitudes because I have seen so much of it in my mother, and I do find some of it in myself.

Marilyn Kane
Joe's sister

You write like you talk. I'm still recovering from your UNC scheduling debacles. When you describe what it's like in waiting rooms, and when chemo is administered, I feel like I'm in the room with you.

Christopher Woods
Family Friend

Dear Cora,

On Friday afternoon I read your book about Joe. My emotions moved from sorrow to rejoicing and all manner of places in between. Some of it was truly heart wrenching and other parts cause me to feel warmth and love. Oh, you did an exceptional job with it; the detail was unbelievable.

Nurtia Bullock
Family Friend

It was great. Now I'm totally invested in Joe. I need to know what happens. You are a great writer. You went through the same thing my sister and I went through with our mother who died January 19, 2015 after a two year ordeal. We did not have the long distances to travel like your family has had. We just had to travel from the Triangle to Winston-Salem. Don't end the book here. When my mom had her stroke September 2012, the stroke destroyed her short term memory more than her physical ability. We placed her in a facility like your father-in-law for a one month stay to improve her diet. On the first day she fell and broke her leg. She never remembered her stroke or breaking her leg. She did not know why she was bed ridden. Every time she had to go to the bathroom we had to explain to her that she could go in her diaper. She threatened to divorce my stepfather and take him, my sister and I out of her will because we would not help her to the bathroom.

Rick Felker
Family Friend

Chapter 1

You hem me in behind and before, and you lay
your hand upon me.
- Psalm 139:5

Each family will have their own unique experience with the dying process of a parent or loved one. Some families will draw close together while others will be splintered for eternity. How we approach the last months, weeks, or days of a life can define who we are as a family. Will cries of desolation fill the air as the last breath is taken? Or will hands be held and prayers raised for our loved one as they separate from this world and move into the spiritual realm? As I write this, death has not yet come, but is knocking on the door of Joe, my father-in-law. His breathing has become labored and more time is spent in bed passing back and forth from the physical to the spiritual realm.

When I was young, I never understood that when you married, you also married into the family. All I knew at the time was that I was in love and I meant it when I said, "For as long as we both shall live." I never realized that for the rest of my life, I would be embedded into my husband's family, along with all its complexities. Now, as I look back over these thirty-six years, I can honestly say that I have been truly blessed to have my husband's family; a family that I now call my own.

Jay and I met in La Grange, North Carolina in the fall of my junior year at East Carolina University. He was living with a good friend, Warren Brothers, a couple miles outside of town. My sorority sister, who was dating Warren, wanted to introduce us. So one Friday evening, Jackie and I drove over to La Grange to surprise them with a visit.

Jay and Warren lived in an old farmhouse located right outside of La Grange. Warren's family had been tobacco farmers for several generations and Warren continued to work the fields with his family. Several years earlier, his family purchased this house that was just down the street from the main farm. This dilapidated house, which Warren called home, with weeds growing up through the floorboards and an old wood heater, was a great house to host parties. So it was not uncommon to find dozens of Jay and Warren's friends hanging out there on any given night.

It was one of those nights with a party beginning to take place that my world forever changed. Many people don't believe in love at first sight, but there is no way to describe how I felt when I first met Jay. I had just entered the side entrance of the house when I saw a young man coming out of a room with just a towel wrapped around his waist. He had dirty blonde hair, blue eyes, and a surfer's tan. A sensation suddenly came over me, similar to the way you feel when you are plunging down the incline of a roller coaster. I can't describe why I felt this way. It may have been his looks, or just the way he carried himself, but whatever it was, right then and there, I knew I wanted to spend the rest of my life with him.

During that first visit and for the weeks to follow, the desire to be with him only grew. Jay would make the forty-five minute trip to Greenville to see me or I would travel the back roads of Eastern North Carolina just to be with him. And if we couldn't see each other, we were calling each other every chance we could.

Jay was a hard worker who decided early on that he wasn't interested in going to college, but wanted to do something with his hands. He had been a member of the Vocational Industrial Club in high school and had taken several vocational courses at the community college in Kinston. He always had a job either working in the tobacco fields or working for his uncle who owned a heating and air conditioning business. He had lived at home for the first year after graduating from high school and then moved in with Warren. His father wasn't in favor of the move, but Jay was determined it was time to spread his wings and become more independent.

Jay loved to surf and with the beach only a little over an hour away, he could be seen driving his green Volkswagen Beetle down Highway 70 whenever he had the chance. Life was good and between trips to the beach or just hanging out together, we were truly enjoying our newfound romance.

During those first months we found a routine that worked for us. Usually, after my classes on Friday, I would go to Kinston to volunteer at an institution for the mentally handicapped. After my volunteer work, I would make the fifteen minute trip to La Grange for the weekend.

But this routine came to a sudden halt when Warren abruptly married another home town girl and started a family, forcing Jay to move back home. I was still living in a dorm and we were having a difficult time with this sudden change. Jay and I discussed the details and we decided to get married over spring break of my senior year.

We were married on March 3, 1979 in front of a packed church filled with friends and family. After our honeymoon, we moved to a small town about forty-five minutes away from his parent's home. During those early years of marriage, I learned

3

a lot about the family that I would forever call my own.

Joe had been in the military for the majority of his adult life and Argene was a nurse by trade. They had met while she was finishing up nursing school and he was stationed in Norfolk, Virginia. Joe served in the Navy during the Korean War conflict and was a part of the Special Forces in Vietnam. While he was away, Argene worked as a nurse at an institution for the mentally ill and raised Jay and his sister Mary Beth.

I can't imagine a couple with such different personalities. Joe was always on the move and Argene loved to sit and do needlepoint. She loved to be close to her family and he wanted to be left alone. Argene could be content for hours sitting around the table with friends and family talking about her past while Joe didn't want to mention his.

New to the family, I had begun to notice friction between Argene and Joe, but I felt it wasn't my place to ask about it. Jay and I didn't discuss it much and it seemed like a discussion that he wanted to avoid.

After four years of marriage, we had our daughter, Sara. I will never forget the long night before her birth and how Argene stayed with me while waiting for my own parents to arrive at the hospital. My mom and dad lived about two hours away and were waiting for the baby's arrival before making the trip to meet their first grandchild. Jay had worked a twenty-four-hour shift and had just laid down before I went into labor. Once we got to the hospital, it became evident that the labor would probably take all night, so he was given a bed to sleep on while Argene sat with me. As the labor pains grew with no end in sight, she held my hand and distracted me with stories about Jay and his childhood.

Several years later, Joe received a job promotion and they moved from Eastern North Carolina to Columbia, South

Carolina. They found a three-bedroom patio home that was situated at the end of a cul-de-sac. There were about twenty homes in the complex with very close-knit neighbors. The patio home sat on top of a hill that overlooked the first hole of a private golf course. All the houses were connected by a brick wall or breezeway. Joe built a nice-sized deck on the back of his house and placed a plastic roof on it to protect them from misdirected golf balls. On any sunny day you could find Joe sitting on his deck or puttering around his yard.

About the same time, we also moved to my hometown of Durham, North Carolina to be around my mom who had cancer and was in poor health. Even though we had moved farther apart, we continued to spend holidays and occasional weekends together.

After being a part of their family for several years, I began to see major flaws in Joe and Argene's marriage. It seemed like they were arguing a lot. Typically, when an argument would begin, Joe would retreat to his workshop to work on his latest artistic or handyman project.

Joe was a very talented man. He was always experimenting with different forms of art, either painting, stained glass, or wood carvings, just to name a few. During his last decade, he got involved in making golf clubs and became very active in the Golf Clubmakers Association. In the end, he had a workshop that was packed with almost every tool you could think of and parts needed to make golf clubs. I do believe his purchasing of these types of items was another sore spot in their marriage. Argene was very thrifty with money and Joe wasn't. I remember overhearing many tense conversations about the purchases made for his most current hobby.

As the years went by, I often wondered what kept this couple together. They acted like they didn't even like each other, but neither of them ever mentioned divorce. I later learned that Joe had been given away by his mother to some close friends that lived in the same town. His mother had divorced and she felt she couldn't raise all four of her children. So she gave Joe up. He lived with this family until he turned seventeen and then joined the service. I can't imagine the feelings of abandonment he must have felt. He never spoke about this time of his life, but I do believe this experience caused him to have a great sense of loyalty toward his marriage.

Chapter 2

God sets the lonely in families.
- Psalm 68:6

In August of 2002, Argene had a major stroke that ended up leaving her bedridden for the remainder of her life. At first, it looked like she was making progress, but as time went on, she continued to have mini-strokes that left her in an unconscious state. Even though she required round-the-clock care, Joe refused to place her in a nursing home.

About this time, Mary Beth was going through a messy divorce and she ended up moving in with her parents and taking care of Argene. This was a true blessing for everyone. Mary Beth needed a place to stay and Joe had someone to take care of his wife while he continued to work. It was a difficult time for everyone, but the family pulled together to make Argene's life as comfortable as possible until the end. Mary Beth took pride in how she took care of her mother. Even though Argene was confined to the bed for at least three years, she never once acquired a bedsore. I know Jay and his father were extremely grateful for Mary Beth and the excellent care she provided.

On December 31, 2005, Argene died.

Chapter 3

Fathers, do not exasperate your children.
- Ephesians 6:4

After Argene's death, I discovered a lot about Joe and his feelings about being a father. After being used to spending most holidays and many weekends together, I was truly surprised when Joe didn't even call to wish Jay a happy birthday. And it wasn't only his son who he ignored. I will never forget being in Palm Springs, California on Mary Beth's birthday. We were on the top of a mountain looking down on the city. For some reason, I thought about Joe and wanted to call and share this moment. After telling him where we were and the incredible view we were experiencing, I reminded him about Mary Beth's birthday. I was truly surprised that he hadn't even given it a thought.

I never really paid close attention to how Jay and his father related to each other. Jay never talked much about his childhood except when he mentioned doing things with his friends or his mother's family. The only positive memories he shared regarding his father centered on the trips made up north to spend time with Joe's family. Each year around Thanksgiving they would pack up the car and make the twelve-hour trip up to Patterson, New Jersey to spend the holiday with distant relatives. Jay always had great stories to tell about their train rides into New York City to take in Broadway shows. He particularly liked walking around Times Square and watching the masses of people flood into the city.

Jay also shared memories about the days when he was a Boy Scout in his father's troop. He has clear memories of camping trips and badge activities where Joe showed favoritism toward other scouts. On many occasions, Joe made a special effort to be involved in the lives of other Boy Scouts at the expense of his own son. It must have really hurt Jay because he left the Scouts when he was only a badge away from earning Eagle Scout rank.

Jay once mentioned to me that Joe had never hugged him. I was surprised by this statement because Joe has always made an effort to hug me when we arrive to or leave his home. After this conversation, I began to notice that Joe only extended his hand to Jay and never reached out for a hug. It makes me very sad to think about the void between the two of them.

It is now clear that there were some major unresolved issues between Jay and his dad. Whenever Joe got mad, the anger always seemed to be directed toward Jay. No matter what good deed Jay did for his dad, it never seemed to be appreciated. This has become clearly evident over the last ten months as we have become more involved in Joe's life. My hope is that God will somehow bring peace between this father and his son.

Chapter 4

Do nothing out of selfish ambition or vain conceit.
- Philippians 2:3

As the months turned into years, Joe seemed to distance himself from both of us. Instead of spending more time together after the loss of Argene, we rarely saw or heard from him. It was evident that he was truly enjoying his independence from family life and had exchanged time with us for a new relationship.

Several years before Argene became sick, she had met a woman named Judy. Judy and Argene had become close friends through volunteer work and church projects. Judy's husband had recently died and she enjoyed coming over to see both Argene and Joe. When Argene became sick, Judy could frequently be found over at the house visiting with her. As time went by, Judy began to spend more time talking with Joe and less time visiting with Argene. So it wasn't a surprise to any of us that after Argene passed away, Joe and Judy became an official twosome.

For the first few years, whenever we would call or come to visit, Joe would be spending time with Judy. Every Saturday night, Joe could be found at Judy's house watching *The Lawrence Welk Show*. And if they weren't at each other's houses, they were spending time eating out or going to the beach.

If Joe was not spending time with Judy, he could be seen out and about in the neighborhood. Most of his neighbors adored him. Joe had become a pleasant fixture on Hillshire Court. He was always eager to fix a pipe, replace a light bulb, or do other odd jobs. He had an infectious smile and kind words for almost everyone. He loved to just come over and share a cup of coffee or invite the neighbors down to sit on the back porch to have a chat.

But as time went by, the relationship began to falter. Judy stopped taking the short trip to Joe's house, but expected him to come when she called. She constantly made excuses to avoid being with him unless she needed something. Joe would complain about how badly he was treated by her one day and turn around and call her the next. But when they were getting along, you would think you were watching a pair of adolescents on their first date. They didn't seem to care if others were around as they cuddled and kissed each other. Clearly, no matter how poorly Judy treated Joe, he loved her.

It was sad to see how he adored her even though she never once went out of her way for him. After Joe was diagnosed with cancer, Judy's true nature became crystal clear. Not once did she come over throughout the entire period that Joe needed someone to encourage him or take him to a doctor's appointment. Some of Joe's neighbors were eager to complain to us about how awful Judy was treating Joe. Even so, Judy and Joe stayed in touch through phone conversations or an occasional visit to her house.

Chapter 5

*There is a time for everything, and a season
for every activity under the heavens: a time to be
born and a time to die.*
- Ecclesiastes 3:1-2

One main thing I have learned from this journey is that death
is a natural part of life and should be embraced instead of
dismissed from conversations. I just picked up a book called
Moving Miss Peggy by Robert Benson. It is a story of the
author's family as they moved their mother into a new place
to live because of her onset of dementia. After reading this
book, I realized that most families aren't prepared to deal with
the inevitable. There is no textbook to teach us how to make
the important decisions that we all eventually come face-to-
face with. But typically, we all fumble through, hoping that
something will occur to just make it all go away.

As we go through this time of Joe's sickness and impending
death, I have often reflected on the commonalities and
differences of how each parent has traveled toward their last
breath. My mom had been sick with cancer for a very long
time. For at least a year before her death, she needed assistance
with daily routines. She pleaded with us to let her live out her
last days in her home. Thankfully, we were able to consent
to her wishes. My brother, sister and I lived within twenty

minutes of her house and on any given day someone would typically go over to check on her.

We also had several home health agencies that provided care for her. Many strangers came to my mom's house, causing us a great deal of anxiety. While some were excellent caregivers, other providers actually stole money and different possessions from her. We were never at peace with this arrangement with strangers, but we knew that it was our only option if my mother was to stay in her home.

The last week of my mother's life was like a walking nightmare. I had been very close to her and my heart was breaking over the approaching passing of not just my mom, but my dear friend. She had slipped into a coma and my brother, who lived in London, was called. Everyone else had been there a couple of days, but it seemed like she was waiting to say goodbye to her oldest son. The morning he arrived, she awoke from her coma and was able to greet him. Late that night, she passed away.

As I reflect back, I will always be grateful that my mom and I were able to share how much we loved each other before she slipped away. The morning of her death, I came by to find her awake and aware of my presence. I drew close to her, holding her hand and caressing it. I leaned over and whispered, "I love you Mom."

In a raspy voice, she said the words that will always be etched into my memory, "I love you too, Cora."

My dad suffered from Parkinson's disease for close to ten years before his death. He married his third wife, Barbara, around the same time of his diagnosis. Barbara was the love of his life. He truly adored her and she him. They lived in Wilmington, North Carolina in a golfing community. His last couple of years were spent playing golf and going over to my brother's cottage on the beach and completing a puzzle as he looked over the seashore. He was happy and at peace with his life.

In August of 2010, Dad was diagnosed with lung cancer. Because of the Parkinson's and his declining health, the doctors only recommended radiation. In October, he finished the six weeks of radiation and went home. Thanksgiving Day, he stood at the head of the table and said grace. After he finished his meal, he got up and went to his room to lie down. Not knowing that he would never be able to get up again.

A week before Dad died, hospice became involved and gave us the support we needed to allow him to pass on. I will never forget the compassionate manner in which these nurses took care of my father and helped Barbara understand the importance of giving my father permission to die. It was such a sharp contrast to the health care providers that we had used for my mom's care.

Some memories become instilled in our minds forever. The night before Dad's death holds such memories. I was sleeping across the hall from the bedroom where he was asleep in the hospital bed we had brought in. I could hear his breathing getting shallower and shallower. Then, I heard the creaking of his bed as Barbara joined my father and cradled him in her arms. Through tears, she sobbed, "Jim, it is okay to go. I will be fine, and Millie, your little dog, will be fine as well." She lay there for hours, repeating these words through muffled tears, knowing this would probably be the last night of his life. The next day, surrounded by most of his children and the woman he loved so much, he stopped breathing.

Chapter 6

Honor your father and mother.
- Ephesians 6:2

It seems like just yesterday when I answered the phone and it was Joe. He sounded disoriented as he told me the news.

"Cora, I just wanted to call you and Jay and let you know that I have lung cancer."

The words were like a punch to my gut. It only seemed like yesterday that my dad had been buried with this dreaded disease. Joe continued, "I don't want to bother you with this and don't worry about coming down here. My neighbors will take care of me."

It took me a minute or two to process what he was saying and how our lives would be radically changed from this moment on. I couldn't remember the last time Joe called us, and for all we knew he was doing fine. I couldn't believe that he didn't want us to come. Did he really think that he could totally rely on his neighbors at this time? Speechless, I gave the phone to Jay and allowed him to talk with his dad about the details.

Once Jay hung up the phone, we discussed the situation and how Joe had appeared unreasonable. He had been demonstrating signs of the onset of dementia for some time.

A couple months prior to the lung cancer diagnosis, one of his neighbors had called us to share her concerns. She had stated that Joe was becoming more opinionated about certain issues regarding the neighborhood. She also shared that she had recently seen him wandering around the neighborhood with the look of a lost puppy. Jay had been very concerned after this conversation and made a trip down to South Carolina to check on his father. Other than being a little disoriented, Jay found his father in good spirits.

One of the first calls Jay made was to the pulmonary specialist that Joe had been seeing. Joe hadn't told the health care providers about us. He had told them that he had children but they were just too busy with their own lives to care about him. That was as far from the truth as you could get, but since he had decided to live an independent life without including us, he must have just assumed we felt the same. I could tell from Jay's expression that the nurse was overjoyed to hear from a family member. Jay told me later that she was yelling, "Thank you, Jesus!" and was actually crying.

Knowing that Joe had pushed us away for all these years made it extremely difficult for us to ignore our feelings of abandonment. But as they say, the apple doesn't fall far from the tree. Joe had always been loyal to keeping his marriage in place, no matter how he had felt about Argene. In the same way, Jay was going to make sure his father received the best care until the day he died.

From the beginning, we knew we needed to act in a compassionate manner. I truly believe in the verse, "Honor your father and mother," which is the first commandment with a promise, "…that it may go well with you and that you may enjoy long life on the earth." I find it very cool that God promises us a long life that we can enjoy if we honor Him by honoring the parents that He gives us.

As soon as we learned about Joe's condition, we began traveling the four hours to his home and taking him to his different doctor appointments. We also got to know his neighbors and began to hear more of their concerns. The more we talked with the professionals and people he was the closest to, the clearer it became to us that Joe's mind was not functioning on all cylinders.

One neighbor informed us that Joe was coming to her house more and more and being forceful about being let in. She noticed that he needed lots of assistance and was forgetting important doctor appointments. She also shared that Joe was becoming increasingly agitated with her when she refused to take him because of other obligations.

During this conversation, she shared how Joe found out he had lung cancer in the first place. Apparently, Joe had been watching a commercial by a law firm regarding mesothelioma. The law firm was soliciting people who had worked with asbestos to contact them to see if they were entitled to trust funds that had been set up for people who suffered from this disease.

Joe called the law firm and someone came to his house and spoke with him. In order to file a claim, they referred him to a pulmonary specialist who did an X-ray of his lungs. Sure enough, there was a tumor in his upper right lung. They also found the outer lining of his lungs to be coated with asbestos. Because of the cancer and the coating of asbestos, the law firm sent Joe the paperwork to file claims. But by this time, Joe was unable to understand what to do with the unopened documents from the lawyers.

It was amazing how many people were sincerely glad to meet us when we started coming down to South Carolina. From the doctors to the neighbors, everyone had a story to tell and appeared extremely relieved that someone was taking responsibility for Joe. By this time, Joe hardly ever spoke about Judy. She would call every once in a while but rarely made an effort to come by. It was a true blessing that Joe had neighbors and health care providers that cared deeply for him. The one event that provoked his neighbor to harass Joe into calling us centered on a scheduled positron emission tomography—commonly known as a PET scan—that he totally forgot about. This put everyone on high alert, including his general practitioner.

Chapter 7

I will fear no evil, for you are with me.
- Psalm 23:4

During this first month of our unchartered journey, we were not sure how to address the major issues we were encountering. We began by driving down from North Carolina to take Joe to his first appointment on March 4. I remember that well because March 3 was our thirty-fifth wedding anniversary. We ended up at Ruby Tuesdays, which I like for lunch, but not for celebrating thirty-five years of marriage. I also remember that we ordered a steak which was not very good. Oh well, I just have to remember what Forrest Gump's mother said, "Life was like a box of chocolates. You never know what you're gonna get." That was becoming so true for all of us as we stumbled through these unexplored waters.

Joe was a stubborn man who loved his independence. Up to this point, he had been able to take care of his financial and personal needs and just wanted to be left alone. He hadn't had a car accident, and even though he got lost while driving to places in the area that he had been to many times, he was able to get himself home eventually. Only once to our knowledge had he left a burner on which caused the alarm to go off. When we asked about the doctors' appointments, he stated that his neighbors would help him. He didn't believe this should be a burden to them because he had helped them many times in the past with handyman projects. Joe just couldn't accept the fact that he actually did need our assistance.

About this time, we started noticing that Joe would only refer to us as "you people." It was like we were strangers to him and not his family. At first it upset me, but over time I began to find humor in this expression. If this is what he thought of us, then we would just have to accept it. Jay, Mary Beth and I now have a standing joke that when Joe dies we are going to put in his obituary, "Joe Darrah, survived by You People."

One of the first major signs of a person experiencing dementia shows up at a doctor's appointment for a new condition. They are taken to a place where they have never been before and asked questions that to them, can sound like a different language. The individual has to find cards in their wallet that may not be easily located because of the infrequency of their use. Then they are given forms that ask for a medical history that could have been long forgotten. Lastly, the patient is asked to wait for the doctor which can cause tremendous anxiety and confusion.

I do believe that as Joe attended more and more appointments, he became more and more grateful for someone to be with him. Just having someone to help redirect him when necessary or find the insurance card that was stuck behind another card made a huge difference. I can't name the number of times he thought he didn't have his military ID or insurance card. Over time, we learned if we could bring him some interesting reading material, find a comfortable seat for him to sit in, and fill out the necessary forms, he could settle down and relax.

The first major appointment we took him to was to have a bronchial scope placed in his lung. Before the procedure, the doctor noted that Joe had an abnormal heartbeat and needed to see a cardiologist. After visiting the cardiologist and being placed on medicine, he was scheduled for the outpatient procedure.

We had planned for Joe's sister, Marilyn, to fly down and take him to this appointment, but realized that it was in a hospital that she had never been to before and it was just easier if Jay, Marilyn and I did this together. So we all got up around 6:30 in the morning and made our way to downtown Columbia. As we found our way through the maze of the hospital corridors, Joe reminded me of a small child who was content to know that someone else was in control. It was then that I knew that we had found our purpose for as long as Joe needed us.

After the procedure, the doctor came out into the waiting room. "Mr. Darrah, I want to inform you that your father is having a difficult time with the anesthesia and has been moved to a recovery room where he is being closely monitored. The bronchial scope has confirmed the diagnosis of stage three lung cancer. There is a lymph node that has been impacted by the cancer. The survival rate is very low unless he has his entire right lung taken out and then has radiation and chemotherapy to address the lymph node. I recommend that you speak to a surgeon about this procedure."

We were then directed to a different waiting area where we tried to digest the information we were just given. Finally, after waiting for about an hour, an attendee assisted Joe out into the waiting room. Other than being disoriented, he seemed to be okay. After driving Joe home, we sat outside and made some calls to close family members to discuss the information the doctor had shared. Everyone seemed to be in agreement that since Joe had a heart condition and dementia he should not have his entire right lung removed.

Even though we didn't think Joe should undergo such a serious operation, we didn't see the harm in going to hear what the surgeon had to say. So we scheduled an appointment for the next week and drove back home to North Carolina to consider how we would approach this diagnosis.

The following week, Mary Beth and I drove back down to take Joe to the surgeon's appointment. We left early one morning and had enough time to pick Joe up from his home and drive to the doctor's office. We walked Joe into the large waiting room and found a seat near a spacious window. Joe seemed happy to have us with him and told us how much he appreciated our company.

After about a thirty-minute wait, we were ushered back to the doctor's office. Then, after another fifteen minutes, the surgeon and a nurse walked in.

"Mr. Darrah, how are you feeling today?"

"They tell me that I have lung cancer, but no one is doing anything about it," Joe answered as he pointed to his upper right chest area.

The surgeon looked up at us. "Mr. Darrah, I would like to discuss having your right lung surgically removed."

At this point, I became agitated and felt the need to ask, "Can you please tell us how this surgery will impact Joe's quality of life?"

"He will need to be on oxygen and probably will not feel like doing a lot of physical activities. Mr. Darrah seems to be in good physical condition and I personally would rather perform surgery on a healthy eighty-three-year-old man than an unhealthy sixty-five-year-old man."

I was now becoming angry. It was like he didn't even consider the fact that Joe had dementia, even though we had discussed this and it was apparent from Joe's responses to his questions. And just the previous week Joe had difficulty with the anesthesia during a very simple procedure. Whatever happened to health care that looked at the overall quality of life instead of trying to make a buck?

Chapter 8

"For my thoughts are not your thoughts, neither are your ways my ways," declares the LORD.
- Isaiah 55:8

The next couple of months didn't improve my thoughts about how the health care industry deals with individuals with multiple diagnoses. Jay, Mary Beth and I wanted Joe to enjoy his last year or so without chemotherapy, surgery, or radiation. I have strong feelings about this due to how both of my parents died. Both had cancer and both went through treatment that only sped up the dying process. My mom had a radical procedure where they inserted a medal prong in her neck before giving her radiation which caused burns to her neck and my dad had radiation that caused him to become extremely tired and weak.

I have yet to hear a doctor state, "Due to age and severity of the patient's present cognitive conditions, let us consider palliative care." I know that doctors are supposed to offer services until the end, but I don't think they should make family members feel guilty if they choose to refuse them. And this is how we felt when we had to explain why we were choosing to go the route of quality of life over radical procedures.

I had heard great things about the University of North Carolina's new cancer treatment center and wanted Joe to receive care there. We were hoping that if he did decide to accept treatment, he could live with us. I had recently retired and had the time to take Joe to his medical appointments and help take care of his other needs.

It is funny how you play out events in your head and think you know exactly how the situation will evolve. Then, as time goes by, you realize you were totally wrong. This is exactly what happened to the idea of Joe coming to North Carolina to live.

We made an appointment for early May and went down to South Carolina and brought Joe back to stay at our house. We have a three-bedroom house, one bedroom downstairs and two upstairs. Our adult daughter has been living with us and uses the entire upstairs for an art study and bedroom. We recently purchased a twenty-four-foot camper with a comfortable full size bed, small kitchen, and bathroom. I placed clean sheets on the bed and put some of Joe's favorite beverages in the refrigerator. We thought this would allow him to have his own space where he could watch his television shows and have some peace and quiet.

At that point, I thought I had it all figured out. Even though Joe didn't seem that happy about the situation, it appeared like we could make it work. The next morning when he came into the house, I could tell that he was pretty anxious. We didn't question him too much about it and figured he would get used to the arrangement.

My oldest daughter, who is a practicing nurse, joined Joe and I as we made our way to his appointment at UNC. Sara has a lot of medical knowledge and I thought she could help us with interpreting test results. The new medical facility that houses the cancer unit was easy to find and very accessible. As we walked through the glass doors, we entered an open lobby with high ceilings and glass walls that led into a central courtyard. Sara, Joe and I followed the signs to the receptionist's desk with a packet of medical forms. Once I had the attention of the woman behind the desk, I stated, "We are here with Joe Darrah. He has an oncology appointment."

The woman gazed at her computer screen and then looked up. "I am sorry but his appointment has been cancelled."

For a moment I was speechless. She continued. "The hospital is using a new system that calls the patient's cell phone number to verify the appointment. It looks like from the information that I have here that someone cancelled."

In an anxious voice I stated, "I did not receive a call from the system and if the system did call Joe, he wouldn't have understood how to respond." Joe probably has one of the oldest cell phones still working and only knows how to answer a phone call or dial a number. Nothing more than that. "He has come all the way from South Carolina for this appointment and it would be very difficult to reschedule it."

It was clear from how she focused on the screen in front of her that she was diligently working on fitting Joe into an appointment slot. As I looked over at Joe, I could tell that he wasn't sure what was happening. Finally, after a couple of awkward minutes, we were directed to the second floor to wait for the next opening.

As we were sitting in the waiting room of the cancer unit, I couldn't help but observe the people around me. Many had lost their hair and others had ports with tubes hanging from their clothes. Most had loved ones surrounding them as they waited for the next treatment or news from the doctors. I remember one older man with his wife's arm wrapped around his shoulders. When a particular doctor walked past, he stopped to give the cancer patient a hug and tell him congratulations on his latest test results. I then noticed a frail woman with gray hair in a wheelchair sitting near us. There were several family members of many generations talking among each other. It touched my heart to see how they reached for her hand or addressed her by name.

As I took in all my surroundings I was overwhelmed with gratitude for my own health. I had to admit that I have no way of understanding what individuals with cancer or other life-threatening diseases go through on a daily basis. Besides the horrific pain or ongoing internal fear, these individuals have lost all control of their present or future and are forced into a dependency on others.

I peered over at Joe, who was sitting there flipping through his wallet looking for his military ID. When we registered, the receptionist asked to make a copy of it. She then gave it to Sara with instructions to go to the payment department to clear up a bill of close to five thousand dollars that was sent to Joe before he even came for his first appointment. As we were waiting, I had to reiterate to him that Sara had it and would bring it back. He seemed very confused and was not able to stop looking for it until she returned. This event had a long-lasting impact on his memory, for weeks afterwards, he would tell people that his military ID was missing.

After Joe settled down, I looked to see what kind of literature was available to read. I found a small brochure about palliative care and flipped through it. I couldn't help but question my motives when thinking about declining treatment for Joe. Could modern medicine truly save him from cancer without jeopardizing his quality of life? And will the dementia be considered by the medical professionals when determining the best treatment plan?

My thoughts were suddenly interrupted by the nurse calling

for Joe to join her at the open door. We were ushered into a room with a couch and a desk with a chair. Because Joe's appointment had been accidently cancelled, it was clear that people were scrambling to get information and determine what course of action should be taken. A physician assistant started the appointment by asking lots of historical questions. Joe sat there and pointed to his upper right chest area stating that he had lung cancer and no one was doing anything about it. The PA was very patient with Joe as she asked questions and filled out her forms. She recommended that Joe be seen by a geriatric social worker to assess his ability to handle treatment. I totally agreed and was excited that someone might attempt to address both the dementia and lung cancer.

Talk about being disappointed! I was a special educator for over three decades and completed lots of interviews and surveys that addressed adaptive behavior and the emotional wellbeing of my students. I was shocked when this social worker came in and started asking Joe questions about his present status and if he understood the treatment options. Joe answered the questions but it was clear that he either didn't understand what was being asked or the dementia had interfered with him knowing the truth. She had asked Joe if he ate three meals a day and he told her he did. Since spending time with him, we had noticed that Joe would forget if he had eaten at all. The social worker also asked about the medications he takes but Joe was unable to name a single one. When the social worker was leaving the room, I had to stop her and make sure she knew that most of what Joe had said wasn't true.

Finally, the doctor came in and looked over Joe's chart. He confirmed that Joe had stage three lung cancer and he wanted him to have an MRI to see if the cancer had metastasized to the brain. He scheduled the MRI for the following Monday evening and a follow-up for the next Tuesday afternoon.

Chapter 9

Trust in the Lord and do good.
- Psalm 37: 3

After the appointment, all Joe talked about was going back home. Nothing we could do or say helped distract him from his desire to be back at 121 Hillshire Court. More and more, he seemed like a fish out of water struggling to make his way back into his familiar pond. Mary Beth ended up driving him back to South Carolina where he stayed for the week as he waited for his next appointment.

The next weekend, Jay and I made the four-hour voyage to retrieve his father for his MRI at UNC. Once we got back to Durham, I again placed clean sheets on the bed in the camper and made sure Joe had everything he needed. Never once did he tell me that he just didn't want to be out there. Instead, the next morning he was found lying on the couch in our family room with the bedspread draped over his body. After letting him know it was okay to tell me the truth, he admitted that he felt claustrophobic and couldn't stand being so confined. So we brought all his personal items into our bedroom and prepared the camper for us.

That day seemed to last forever with no real plans until his appointment. Once we made our way to Chapel Hill, we realized we were running a couple of minutes late and had to do some speed walking to get to the receptionist desk. Jay was first to the desk.

"My father Joe Darrah has an appointment for an MRI."

The receptionist stared at his computer. "I am sorry but his appointment has been cancelled."

Talk about feelings of anger brewing under the surface. I just had to butt in. "I scheduled this appointment last week and have not received any message that it had been cancelled."

Without even looking up from the computer, he replied, "I can fit him in but he will have to wait until the technicians get back from their dinner break."

None of us were happy about the situation, but what could we do? Jay sat there flipping through magazines, I was playing games on my phone, and Joe was searching through his wallet for his military ID. Every once in a while Jay would tell me that we were leaving and boy did I want to go but we knew we had to stay. What choice did we have?

The next afternoon, Jay and I took his father to see the doctors one more time so we could discuss his prognosis. Joe was getting extremely antsy and didn't like being away from home. This is such a clear sign of dementia. It is literally like taking candy away from a small child and telling them to be happy. It just doesn't work. And, of course, when we got to the hospital, the appointment had again been cancelled and we had to sit an extra hour before they could see us. As I sat in the waiting room, I spotted many of the same individuals from the previous week. My heart broke for these families that were living from waiting room to waiting room.

None of us were in the best of moods when we entered the doctor's office. It appeared that Joe was the last patient and that everyone was ready to go home. Two doctors came in; one was in charge of radiation and the other in charge of chemotherapy. The doctor in charge of chemotherapy gave us his treatment plan, chemo for six weeks. The radiologist stated that the radiation would also be six weeks. He even had the audacity to tell Joe that without surgery and only radiation and chemo, he could heal him. I was shocked that he could make such a bold statement. By this time it was evident that Joe was thinking about having treatment but it sure wasn't going to be in North Carolina. We thanked the doctors and told them that more than likely Joe would not be treated at UNC. I could tell they were a little put off, but they weren't overly pushy.

Chapter 10

If one falls down, his friend can help him up. But pity the man who falls and has no one to help him up!
- Ecclesiastes 4:10

That night will go down as one of the most bizarre events of this entire journey. On the way home from the hospital, Joe kept pleading to go back to South Carolina. I had plans for the next day and intended on driving him back on Thursday.

Joe suggested, "How about looking up the train schedule?"

I could tell he was almost in tears. "I will look into it when we get back home."

After looking up the times the train left Durham and arrived in Columbia, I approached Joe. "I found only one train that leaves at 9:00pm and arrives at 3:30am."

I don't think he understood that it was 3:30 in the morning because he said with confidence, "I will find someone to pick me up."

"Joe, you do have wonderful neighbors but no one is going to get up in the middle of the night and drive to the train station to pick you up."

I could tell how disappointed he was. "Cora, if you will drive me home tomorrow, I will pay you."

I knew by then that he wasn't going to stop badgering me until I consented. "Let me cancel some appointments and I will take you."

It was amazing how his mood changed once he knew he was going home.

That night, Jay and I ended up sleeping in the camper. Our daughter had a friend staying over and there was no way we could sleep upstairs. I hoped that since Joe was happy to go home the next day we would all have a restful night of sleep.

It just wasn't meant to be. Around 3:15 in the morning, Joe started knocking on the camper door and then yelled. "Cora, Cora, it is time to go."

Jay sat up and yelled back, "Dad, you need to go back to bed. It is only 3:15!"

We could hear Joe's footsteps as he left and went back inside. Now I was wide awake and couldn't stop thinking about the situation. I knew that if Joe was up and ready, there was no way he was going to go back to sleep. So I got up, put on some clothes, and went into the house. He was literally pacing back and forth looking like he was about to cry.

"Joe, give me a couple minutes and I will take you home."

Chapter 11

They are blind guides leading the blind, and if one blind
person guides another, they will both fall into a ditch.
- Matthew 15:14

This was a trip I wasn't looking forward to mainly because I have a sciatic nerve issue in my right leg and if I drive for more than an hour it begins to shoot a pain from my knee up to my right hip. Usually, on long trips like this one, Jay will drive so I don't have pressure on my leg, but he was still working and couldn't always accompany me. When I drive for more than a couple of hours, I can be in excruciating pain; particularly if I have to drive in heavy traffic where I have to use the brakes and gas pedal a lot.

The first part of the trip was actually really nice. A full moon lit up the sky as we made our way down Highway 1. Only a couple of trucks and passenger cars sped by us as we traveled through the night. I was able to use the cruise control and sit back and enjoy the scenery through the shadows of the bright moon.

Joe and I passed the time with interesting conversations about when he was in the service and all the different jobs he held in his lifetime. Recently, I had been hearing more and more stories about how he was wrongly treated in the service and didn't get the recognition he deserved. "I was supposed to be promoted but my commanding officer had me transferred to a different unit. I was the only one in my unit that worked hard and I think he resented it. I was up to be promoted but instead I was transferred. It was just not right!"

Once the conversation took a negative turn, I would draw him into a different topic that he would get excited about. "Joe, tell me about the time you flew over Vietnam and dropped propaganda out of planes."

I found that as long as he could talk about himself, he was content. So for the next couple of hours, we discussed his past, rotating between the pleasant and unpleasant memories.

Finally we were drawing close to Columbia. To get to Joe's house, you have to take Interstate 26 off of Interstate 20. We were getting ready to take this exit when he started yelling, "Do not turn here. Stay on 20!"

"Joe, we have always taken 26 to your house."

"We are going to take 20 until we get to Piney Grove Road!" he shouted at me.

Since I hadn't driven this route in a while, I thought maybe he knew what he was talking about.

Boy, was that a mistake. After missing the exit, my leg was throbbing and I was almost weeping in pain. As each exit came up, he would tell me that it was just a little bit farther. Finally, he saw a road that looked like Piney Grove so we took the exit. When we got off and drove a little ways, he realized we were lost.

I just wanted to cry. We finally pulled into a gas station and Joe wandered inside to ask for directions. While he was trying to find someone to ask, I called Jay to fill him in on our dilemma.

"Jay, we are lost. Your father is inside a gas station asking for directions. I don't want to stress you out but I just need some help using the GPS on my phone."

Joe walked slowly toward the car with a puzzled look on his face. Apparently, the gas station employee couldn't help him. After following Jay's instructions, I was able to insert the address into the phone and the woman's voice began to state the directions to 121 Hillshire Court. We had driven about an hour out of the way. So instead of a four-hour drive, we had now been on the road for five hours. I wasn't looking forward to the drive home but had no intention of staying, no matter how bad my leg hurt.

Before taking him home, he was adamant about going by the bank so he could pull out some money to pay me. It was only 8:30am and I was accustomed to banks opening up at 9:00am. I tried to tell him this, but he only got madder and madder. We pulled into the parking lot and he went inside. He immediately came out telling me that they only served people in the drive-through. So we pulled around to the back and Joe tells the teller that he wants four hundred dollars. Apparently they must know him well, because they completed his withdrawal slip and handed it to me to get him to sign. Then presto, they handed over his money.

After a trip to the gas station to fill up the tank, I took Joe to his little patio home on the golf course. When we arrived, he immediately went across the street to let his neighbors know that he had returned. I went in to use the restroom, did some exercises to prepare my leg for the trip home and headed out. I will never forget the huge smile on his face as I pulled away. Just like a little child at Christmas. What in the world are we going to do?

Chapter 12

Though he brings grief, he will show compassion,
so great is his unfailing love.
- Lamentations 3:32

After a couple of weeks of not hearing from Joe, we received a phone call from Joe's general practitioner's office. Joe was starting to show more symptoms of lung cancer. He was puzzled by the fact that he had a pain in his right chest and no one was doing anything about it. Amazingly enough, Joe called his general practitioner himself and made an appointment. He told him that he didn't want to be in North Carolina but he did want treatment. Even though we were not in agreement, we did understand that this was his life and if he wants treatment, he should receive it. After our conversation, his general practitioner made a referral to South Carolina Oncology Associates.

On June 24, I traveled down to South Carolina to take Joe to his consultation concerning the radiation treatments. He took me out to dinner the night before and I could tell that he truly appreciated my company. At this point in time, I don't think Joe understood the sacrifices we were all making on his behalf. In his mind, I am there and then I am gone. I come back and return into his presence. Never understanding the hours and hours we spent in the car.

The next morning, which was my birthday, we traveled the twenty minutes to the South Carolina Oncology Associates and arrived around 8:00. His neighbor Karen followed us in her own car so she could smoke her cigarettes. Recently, Joe had developed a relationship with this woman that lived across the street. He really enjoyed her company and was elated that she wanted to join us for these appointments as Judy was, by now, largely out of the picture.

After checking in, we found chairs that faced a fish tank that served as a wall between two lobby areas. As we waited for Joe's name to be called, I was compelled to look around at all the people who filled the room. I am sure there were over one hundred people either being checked in or waiting for a doctor. Each patient had to give blood which made it easy to identify the patients from the family members. A volunteer walked by with a Great Dane therapy dog for patients to pet if they chose. The huge dog seemed so out of place that it would have been comical if we weren't all acutely aware of our present circumstances. The first appointment was primarily made up of meeting with the financial department, getting blood work, and checking vital signs. After this was completed we had a gap of time before the meeting with the radiation department.

Since Joe had not had breakfast, we went over to the Waffle House to grab something to eat. Joe seemed a little disoriented when we headed out to the parking lot. When the two of us got into my car, he became insistent that I had left Karen. I reassured him that she had driven separately. He didn't believe me until we saw her car behind us as we headed back for his next appointment.

When we entered the building, we were led to a small sterile room. The nurse came in and shared with us a little bit about radiation and the process Joe will go through. She turned on her computer that had a fifteen-minute presentation on radiation,

the side effects, and what Joe should expect. The video
reminded me of when Jay and I went to the Grove Park Inn
and visited their spa for the day. It explained how the patient
enters the locker room and undresses, places their belongings
in a locker, receives a robe and then goes in for their radiation
treatment. The video downplayed the side effects and I had
to keep reminding myself that this wasn't a spa but a medical
facility. I was a little concerned about how Joe was processing
this information, but it really didn't matter. When I looked over
to check on him, he had fallen into a deep sleep.

After the meeting with the radiologist, we were directed over
to meet the oncologist. I was instantly impressed with how he
spoke to us. He actually seemed to care about Joe as a person.
He was a graduate of Carolina and was interested in knowing
who Joe had seen at UNC. He told us that Joe would receive
six weeks of radiation and six treatments of chemotherapy. The
dose of chemo would only be used to heighten the effects of
the radiation. He would come in for radiation every morning
at 8:00 and spend most of the day on Mondays receiving
chemotherapy. After sharing the information, the doctor gave
us an opportunity to ask questions and actually listened to our
concerns. My main concern had to do with Joe's cognitive
abilities and if chemotherapy would cause his dementia to
worsen. We also asked if Joe would become sick after each
treatment. He shared with us that each person is different and
that we would need to closely monitor Joe after his treatments.

Chapter 13

Who of you by worrying can add a single hour to his life?
- Matthew 6:27

Logistically, I wasn't sure about how this was going to happen, but I knew that if Joe was going to be treated, it would have to be in Columbia. After some conversations with Mary Beth, she decided to use family leave and move down for the summer while her daughter was out of school. She would arrive in early July and stay until the third week of August. I would then come down with Marilyn, stay the last week of treatment and leave after his follow-up appointment.

I didn't know Joe's family up close and personal until a couple of years prior to this calamity. They lived in New Jersey and we lived in North Carolina. We would receive Christmas and an occasional birthday card, but no strong bonds had been formed. Then Hannah, my daughter, moved to New York to pursue a career in contemporary modern dance. Because they lived so close to the city, we began making time to visit them when we came up north to see Hannah.

Marilyn's husband had recently died and she had moved in with her daughter. They loved each other but when an opportunity to travel came up, Marilyn never hesitated to take it. So when I suggested she come with me to spend two weeks with Joe, she jumped on it. I will always be truly grateful to her for her companionship during those weeks.

Life had definitely taken a crazy turn. People who had previously only played minor parts in our lives were now becoming major characters. Joe was now not only the major character, but he was also dictating our days, weeks, and months. If we were not in Columbia spending time with him, we were constantly thinking about how he was doing.

We were also spending lots of money traveling back and forth, and were now starting to feel the financial, as well as emotional toll of this situation. Not knowing how to pay the bills and feeling out of control was difficult for both Jay and I. This was a time we had to just place our faith in God and believe that He would provide.

Chapter 14

Therefore do not worry about tomorrow, for tomorrow will worry about itself. Each day has enough trouble of its own.
- Matthew 6:34

For the next couple of weeks while Mary Beth stayed with Joe, Jay and I felt like we could have a little breather. During this time, I had my yearly mammogram and for the first time, they saw a spot on my right breast. This was particularly alarming because my best friend was being treated for breast cancer and I knew that it was a diagnosis that I was petrified of getting. I immediately called and made an appointment for a more in-depth examination. I decided not to share this information with Jay until I knew something for sure. Life had enough stress without him having to worry about this. Those four days of my life had to be some of the longest I have ever experienced. I couldn't think of anything but having breast cancer. For the first time throughout this journey, I had some idea of what it must be like to have this dreaded disease.

This is what I wrote in my journal as I waited to be called back:

Another waiting room. Durham Diagnostic Imagining. My stomach has been fluttering for days. I had bizarre dreams last night. Some showing breast cancer and others not. I can now say that I don't have a clue what people go through until I go through it myself. Is this a short journey or one that will change my life?

I hear my name being called and follow the nurse to a room where I am to undress and change into a pink smock. I open the door and go into another waiting room where about a half dozen older women sit and stare out into space. I find a chair and join the women with the pink smocks. No one looks at each other. No small talk, just a strained silence as we wait for our fate to be told.

Finally, I hear my name and follow the technician down a long hallway to a room that looks very similar to a doctor's office. There before me is an ultrasound machine that will determine my future. I lay down on the bed and opened up my smock to expose my right breast. At first the technician was very quiet as she applied the gel and started moving the probe over my skin. Then, nonchalantly she states that it is just a benign cyst. I can hardly believe my ears. The relief of knowing that I don't have breast cancer comes rushing through my body. One minute, I could be headed to a time of suffering and the next, I am carefree. A sense of gratitude toward God overwhelms me.

As I pulled out of the parking lot, I called Jay. "I just wanted to let you know that I just left the doctor's office. Last week when I had my yearly mammogram, they saw a spot on my breast."

There was silence for a minute. "Why didn't you tell me?"

"With everything that we are going through with your father, I just wanted to know one way or another before adding another ounce of unneeded stress to your life. Anyway, it is only a benign cyst. I am fine, I love you, and I will see you tonight."

"I love you, too," he states before he hangs up.

Chapter 15

Houses and wealth are inherited from parents.
- Proverbs 19:14

On July 19, we traveled back down to Columbia while Mary Beth took a break from her father and went home for the weekend. On our way down, we discussed how we needed to start cleaning out some rooms while we were there. We knew that there would be a time, sooner rather than later, that Joe would have to leave his home and either move in with Mary Beth or go to an assisted living community. It was almost like Joe knew deep down that he would have to leave and was tightening his grip on everything. His attitude about keeping all the stuff he had accumulated caused us to make sure he was preoccupied while someone else was working on sorting through it.

The first room we tackled was the office where all Joe's legal and financial papers were kept. Jay began the process by cleaning out several file cabinets and was able to locate many important financial documents. Several years ago, Joe hired a lawyer to complete the paperwork for Jay and Mary Beth to have power of attorney when he was unable to take care of himself. We didn't realize how crucial this document was until we started making financial decisions for Joe. Experience has demonstrated over and over again that without power of attorney, Jay would not have been able to help his father through this incredibly difficult time.

After Jay finished cleaning Joe's office, he decided to start working on removing the debris that cluttered the workshop floor. So the next morning while Mary Beth and I took Joe to his chemotherapy appointment, Jay loaded a ton of junk from Joe's workshop and hauled it to the dump. By this time, it was pouring down rain but it didn't deter Jay from his mission. I wish to this day that I took a picture of the workshop space before we started this endeavor. The mountain of clutter and stuff that had to be moved seemed like an impossible task that only brought on a sense of despair for all of us.

Chapter 16

When Jesus landed and saw a large crowd, he had
compassion on them and healed their sick.
- Matthew 14:14

South Carolina Oncology has a floor designated for only chemotherapy. When patients enter this area, they have their blood taken to check their platelets before they can go in for treatment. They are also weighed. Joe weighed 148 pounds. Six pounds less than last week. A couple of years prior to this, Joe had gone on a gluten free diet and lost around twenty pounds. He sure could use those pounds now.

After being weighed, we walked around the corner, and saw the lab where they mix the chemicals for each patient. We then entered a huge room that was about the size of a school gymnasium. In the center of the room was the nurses' station which was very accessible to the patients. The back wall had huge windows that looked out over a cluster of pine trees. There were rows and rows of recliners lined up facing these windows. Several chairs for family members were scattered near the recliners.

As I gazed around I noted that most of the people receiving treatment were either reading or watching a movie on their iPad. Nurses were busy checking on patients and volunteers were asking if anyone needed anything. One older man began talking to the family next to Joe. He stated that he was a cancer survivor and that he loved coming here to encourage others that were in similar circumstances to where he was a couple of years ago.

I was very impressed with the compassion of the nurses and volunteers. Joe was very relaxed as the nurse came over and inserted his IV. We had brought a booklet for Joe to read on the endless ways baking soda can be used. Every time he picked it up and skimmed through it, he acted like it was the first time he had seen it. During the first couple of chemo treatments he was as happy as a clam if he had that baking soda booklet to help pass the time.

While Joe was receiving his chemo, Mary Beth and I were able to talk with a social worker to seek out advice on how we should proceed. Joe's dementia was getting worse and we knew that after his treatment was completed, he would be on his own once again. The social worker's only recommendation was to contact VA services. She gave me a phone number that I called later, but it didn't really lead to any helpful answers. Feeling uncertain of how to make sure Joe's needs were met, I now more than ever felt we were walking aimlessly down a road without a map or destination. No one knew how Joe would tolerate the treatment or how it would impact his memory and most importantly, if he could continue to live on his own.

Chapter 17

Rejoice in the Lord always, I will say it again: Rejoice!
- Philippians 4:4

While Joe continued his treatment, I sat with him as he read through his baking soda pamphlet. It was evident that he enjoyed spending time flipping through the pages and sharing the many valuable uses of this product. While he was preoccupied, I noticed a woman sitting next to Joe. I am not sure why, but I had a strong desire to start a conversation with her. So, I made my way to a chair on the other side of Joe. "Hi, I am here with my father-in-law. He is enjoying his reading and I was wondering if you wanted some company."

The woman smiled. "Sure, come sit down."

Trying not to be too forward I asked, "So what brings you here?"

Without hesitation the woman shared, "I have lung cancer. I have already been through chemotherapy and radiation. I was told about two months ago that the cancer was now in my back. I am here to receive an injection that will hopefully slow down the progression of the cancer."

"I am so sorry."

Thinking that she would not want to talk about it, I tried to consider what to say next. But before I could open my mouth and change the subject she continued. "I have a daughter and two grandchildren that are living with me. My daughter had a rough time with the birth of her second child and before I realized it, she was taking my pain medication. Now she is an addict and stealing from me. I know I need to kick her out of the house but I am not sure how I can take care of the children."

I was now in a state of shock and didn't know what to say. Just about this time a nurse came over to her and I moved back over toward Joe.

The nurse stated to her, "I just came from talking to the doctor. He needs you to make an appointment to discuss the test results from your brain scan." As the nurse administered the injection, she asked, "Did someone come with you today?"

Turning away from us she whispered, "No, I came by myself."

I was almost glad when my phone began to ring. "Hello," I quietly said into the receiver.

"Cora, I am about twenty minutes away," Jay stated. "Can you please meet me in the parking lot?"

"Sure, I will be there."

After I gave Joe and Mary Beth a hug goodbye, I walked toward the elevator and waited for the doors to open. I couldn't stop thinking about the woman I had just met and quietly said a prayer for angels to look over her and her family.

Once I got off the elevator, I made my way through the lobby, past the gift shop toward the main entrance. I passed several people being brought in by ambulance laying on gurneys. Two police officers were walking a prisoner into the building. Older people using walkers slowly moved toward the line to check in. I couldn't help but notice the diversity of the people that filled the lobby and waiting rooms and was convinced that cancer definitely doesn't discriminate.

As I walked through the main doors, I noticed the rain had picked up and found a place under the awning to keep from getting wet. A woman who apparently was waiting for a ride approached me. After my recent conversation, I wasn't sure if I wanted to hear what she had to say. Her southern accent made it difficult to understand her words. "Must be something in the water in my town."

"Why do you think that?" I couldn't help but ask.

"Lots of my kin have cancer."

"I am sorry to hear that," I said, looking out over the parking lot.

"My cat even has it," she stated looking right at me.

"How do you know your cat has cancer?" I asked.

"Because his ears are falling off."

Just about that time, I could see Jay's black truck pull through the parking lot and swing up to the entrance. Not knowing what to say, I moved toward the truck and shouted back, "Have a good day."

It was hard to shake off the conversations that I had with the women I spoke to that day. It almost made me appreciate how well Joe was doing and made me think how much worse our situation could be.

Chapter 18

Trust in the Lord with all your heart.
- Proverbs 3:5

Joe's memory loss was becoming more and more evident. Each day, reality was slipping further away and being replaced with a foggy cloud of confusion. Mary Beth shared with us that after we left, Joe didn't remember Jay being there at all. He hadn't remembered how Jay had taken the TV dish off of the roof due to termination of his Dish network service. This led to Joe becoming hysterical when the service provider kept sending him bills and asking for the dish to be returned, which Jay did. No matter how many times we tried to explain that the dish belonged to the company and it needed to be returned, he came to conclusion that he had been robbed.

Joe was also spending a lot of time trying to locate keys and other objects that he had put down. Sometimes the keys would be hanging off his key chain that was hooked to his pants. Other times, he would reach for his phone to change the television channel or the remote to turn up the heat in the house.

Even though the dementia was impacting his cognitive abilities, physically, Joe was tolerating the radiation and chemotherapy surprisingly well. The only major side effect he was experiencing was a sore throat. The doctors had said that there would be a chance that Joe would have difficulty swallowing due to where the radiation was being applied. For some reason, the radiation didn't affect Joe like it did most. He only complained every once in a while with the phrase, "It's hell getting old."

One morning I received a call from Mary Beth. I could tell that she was a little shook up. "What's wrong?"

"I want to let you know what happened last night. I got up around 11:30 to take my dog outside to use the bathroom. When I came back in, I noticed that there was a light on in Daddy's room. When I walked past, he was pointing a gun at me."

"What!" I cried into the phone.

She continued. "I told him to put the gun down. He did seem a little shaken up that he had a gun pointed at me. He told me that he didn't hear me go out and didn't know who was making the noise."

"Mary Beth, we need to take the gun away from him. Do you think you can hide it from him until we get down there?"

"I will try, but he seems adamant about having it in his bedside table."

The next weekend, Jay went down and was able to take the bullets out of the gun without Joe knowing it. He also locked the gun so that Joe would have to actually unlock it before trying to use it. Joe also had a gun safe in his bedroom closet that contained at least five additional guns. Thankfully, he couldn't remember the combination and when he asked, we were able to change the conversation. Our hope was that he would never be able to get the gun safe open again. Life had sure gotten crazy quick!

Chapter 19

Dishonest money dwindles away, but he who gathers money little by little makes it grow.
- Proverbs 13:11

About this time, we were realizing that more money was going out than coming in. Mary Beth had taken a leave of absence from her job and needed to be compensated for her time down in Columbia. It was becoming more evident that Joe could not be left alone and would need assistance which would cost money that he didn't have in the bank. So Mary Beth made an appointment with Joe's financial advisor to have some money taken out of his investment account. When they arrived, the agent introduced himself and then asked, "Can you please tell me how we can help you?"

Joe seemed confused about why they were there, so Mary Beth spoke up. "My father has lung cancer and I had to take a leave of absence to come and take him to his treatments. He needs money taken out of his account to pay my expenses."

Joe then pointed at his chest. "They tell me that I have lung cancer but no one is doing anything about it."

The agent smiled at Joe and then asked, "How much money do you want to take out of your account?"

Hesitant to answer, Mary Beth stated, "How about five thousand dollars?"

Joe looked at Mary Beth. "Let's take six thousand dollars."

Mary Beth nodded her head in agreement. As they were waiting for the paperwork to be completed, Joe leaned over to Mary Beth and asked, "Where did this money come from?"

She just smiled. "Daddy, this is your retirement money from Underwriters Laboratory."

"Oh, isn't that nice," Joe said with a huge smile.

Chapter 20

But I tell you, love your enemies and pray for
those who persecute you.
- Matthew 5:44

On August 15, Marilyn flew into Raleigh-Durham
International Airport to travel with me down to Columbia for
the last weeks of Joe's treatment. I was surely grateful to have
the company. I doubt I could have spent two weeks with Joe
without support. Jay, Marilyn and I drove down on Sunday. Jay
was off until Wednesday which allowed him to get work done
around the house while we took Joe to his different treatments.
We also brought our dog, Bee, a black and white French
Bulldog.

At this point the money had not been transferred to the bank
and Mary Beth was anxious to pay her bills. Before leaving
on Wednesday, Jay decided to go to the bank to make sure his
name was on Joe's banking account and if the money from his
investment account had been transferred.

When Joe found out what Jay was doing, he became very
upset. He didn't think anyone should be involved with his
finances. Joe then got in his truck and went to the financial
advisor's office. Before long, Jay's phone rings and the agent
requests Jay to come over as soon as possible. Jay told me later

that he had never seen his father so mad. When he entered the office, Joe was sitting in the corner and had a look on his face that could kill. After the agent explained the situation to Joe, he seemed to mellow down and signed the papers that allowed Jay access to his father's account. It was sad to see how hard Joe was trying to cling on to life as he had known it. On the other hand, we were thanking God for Joe's willingness to comply.

Marilyn had a job at a bank back in New Jersey and was good at creating budgets and figuring out what was coming in and what was going out. Joe was on a fixed income with his pension from the military and social security. Amazingly enough, he usually could live within his means.

We did learn how he had been suckered into purchasing some expensive items, though. He had seen a paint gun on TV and just had to have it. So $298.00 later, he had two of these paint guns delivered to his house. The only problem was he already had three of them in his workshop under a bunch of junk. He had also spent $3000.00 for a vacuum cleaner. How crazy is that? Several times when I was there, he was on the phone with someone who wanted to sell him something. It just broke my heart to hear how difficult it was for him to get off the phone without purchasing an item. I can't imagine how many individuals just like Joe have been taken advantage of like this. These telemarketers should be ashamed of themselves!

Chapter 21

"For I know the plans I have for you," declares the Lord.
- Jeremiah 29:11

During this last week of radiation, Joe began to complain about his teeth. He was constantly telling everyone that it felt like something was in between his bottom teeth and he couldn't get it out. I had to laugh when I saw him go back to receive his treatment and was showing the nurse his teeth—you learn to find humor in the strangest of moments. While he was getting his radiation, I went to the receptionist and asked if we could have a doctor check inside Joe's mouth.

Once Joe was finished with his treatment, we were led back to a small examination room. After waiting a couple of minutes, the radiologist came in and asked Joe to tell him what was bothering him. Joe opened his mouth and pointed to where he was experiencing discomfort. The doctor took a quick look and said that the radiation did not cause this issue and he should go see a dentist. I was a little disturbed by the radiologist's bedside manner. The way he approached the situation made us all feel like the teeth were not an issue and shouldn't have been brought to his attention.

One other major concern began to unfold as we spent more time in Columbia. Joe wasn't taking his medication correctly.

He was on several different medications for a variety of issues. We had purchased two different weekly containers that were clearly marked am and pm. On Thursday, I noticed that he had taken Friday's pm as well as Thursday's medication. The next day, I noticed that he had taken the rest of the meds in the container. That afternoon, I sat down with him.

"Joe, I am very concerned that the last two days you have been taking too much medication. I am no longer sure that you can live on your own."

With a pleading tone, Joe said, "Shug, I am perfectly capable of taking care of myself."

"Joe, we are all concerned about how you are going to take care of yourself when we leave. It is not just the medication but the fact that you have gotten lost a couple of times when you have been out driving. If you want to stay here, we would like to hire someone to come and check on you a couple of days a week."

He was clearly against this decision but I knew I had to push it. "Joe, we are all worried about you and we can hardly sleep at night. I would greatly appreciate it if you would consent to this help."

"Okay," he said with a defeated look on his face.

Chapter 22

When words are many, sin is not absent, but he who
holds his tongue is wise.
- Proverbs 10:19

The further into this journey we have traveled, the more we have realized that the individuals who are closest to the family member, providing care and assistance, can also have needs that should be addressed. Since no one taught us how to be a caregiver to a family member with dementia, many mistakes are sure to be made. What happens next is a clear example of why families should be given counseling when faced with this horrendous condition.

Jay drove back down to Columbia on Saturday morning and decided to join us in cleaning up the yard. On the back side of the house facing the golf course was a huge pile of assorted types of wood that Joe had collected whenever he would work on a project. It had become an eyesore that many golfers had complained about, but Joe had refused to clean it up. I think he had become personally attached to it. It reminded me of individuals on some of the hoarding shows on TV. So when Jay began removing it without getting Joe's permission, sparks began to fly.

Jay had pulled Joe's truck up to the wood pile and started

putting the wood in the back. As each piece of wood went in, Joe was becoming increasingly agitated. We didn't realize just how upset he was becoming until we were at the dump. We were placing the wood in the big dumpster when Marilyn called, saying, "I need to let you know that Joe has been hysterical since you left. He keeps telling me that all you two want is his money and wood."

When we got back from the dump, Joe was furious. Joe started yelling at Jay. "You have no business taking my wood. It was not yours to take to the dump. I may need it for a future project!"

Jay countered back, "Dad, we were only trying to help you clear out your backyard. If you don't appreciate our help then maybe I should leave!"

Jay walked away and a silence fell all around us. I could tell he was fed up with the situation and wanted to leave. By this time, I had about reached my limit and was ready to throw in the towel, but knew that Marilyn and I needed to stay.

It seemed that after the blowup and little time apart, the air began to cool.

That afternoon, Jay asked, "Dad, can we move the remaining wood behind the brick wall?"

Joe responded, "Sure, I guess that will be okay."

As soon as the words left his mouth, Jay began moving the wood. Every once in a while, Joe got up to help until he felt the need to rest. I learned a lesson that day: When working with individuals with dementia, it is best to have them be a part of the decision-making process. Something as simple as asking a question can make all the difference in how they will respond.

It had already been a stressful day where emotions had raged.

I have heard the phrase, "When it rains, it pours." And on this particular day it rained bucketfuls!

Later that evening, Jay, Joe and I were sitting on the back porch watching the golfers making their way up the hill to the first green. Karen, Joe's neighbor, came around the corner and pulled up a chair.

"Hey Joe, what are you all doing?"

"Just resting awhile," he said with a huge grin. It was clear Joe loved the attention he received from Karen and was always glad to see her. Even though we knew that there were no romantic feelings between them, they shared a deep friendship. She had told us on occasion that Joe reminded her of her deceased father-in-law. Someone she loved dearly.

After a couple minutes of small talk, Joe stated, "I remember when Jay was in high school and he was hanging out with some people that were no good. One night he came in and we started to argue. I became angry and I remember slapping him across the face."

"Joe, you didn't do that?" Karen asked.

"I sure did," Joe responded.

Joe was sitting there with a smile on his face. He appeared to be boasting about this event to Karen, totally unaware of how this was making Jay or I feel.

Both Jay and I got up to leave at that point, unsure what to say or how to convey to Joe that this was extremely hurtful. No one stopped us and Joe continued to talk about the event to Karen as we walked away.

I knew that his father's words hurt a lot and wasn't sure what to say. "Jay, we need to remember that your father has dementia and this is one of the outcomes of this condition. People will say hurtful things and not even realize it."

"I know, but it still hurts," Jay quietly said as he walked back into the house.

Chapter 23

Forgive and you shall be forgiven.
- Luke 6:37

The next morning we were all sitting out on the porch watching the golfers while enjoying our breakfast. Bee was tied to a run in the backyard. I thought I would let her roam free in the yard as we sat there looking out over the golf course.

Was that ever a mistake! Before I knew it, she had run across a little bridge that connected Joe's yard to the fairway. She then began chasing the golfers and running as fast as she could to the woods beside the greens. I ended up having to run onto the course and persuade Bee to come to me. At first, she wanted nothing to do with coming back to her confined yard; she was delighted with this new world of running around the golfers and into the woods. The golfers were enjoying watching the escapade of my little dog toying with me. Finally, after several bribes with her favorite treat, she came close enough for me to snatch her up into my arms. I then looked up on the deck to see Joe, Marilyn and Jay wipe away the tears of laughter from their faces.

Soon after Bee got loose and was retrieved, Jay left for home taking her with him. It was apparent that Bee needed more attention than we could give her considering the situation with Joe.

The next morning we were sitting back on the porch when Joe asked, "Where is your dog?"

I was tempted to tell him that she had run home but instead replied, "Jay took her home with him."

He looked confused and asked, "Has Jay been here?"

It was crazy that after all the hostility between the two of them over the finances and the wood that Joe had totally forgotten that Jay had been there at all.

Chapter 24

There is a time for everything, a time to embrace
and a time to refrain.
- Ecclesiastes 3:5

I often wondered if we were exaggerating the situation and if Joe truly needed more supervision. Having an objective opinion from a professional who worked with individuals with dementia could only help us with making future decisions.

On Monday, the home health agency sent someone over to interview us and discuss Joe's care. Joe and I were sharing a couch and sitting facing the woman from the agency. I began the conversation by saying, "I appreciate you coming."

The woman had several forms in front of her and was writing as we talked. "What services are you thinking about?"

"We are looking for someone to come in a couple times a week to check if Joe has taken his medication and if he has eaten."

Joe interjected, "Will this person do some cleaning?"

The woman looked at him. "Yes, they can do some light cleaning. They can also take you to appointments if you have a doctor's appointment."

"I don't need anyone taking me anywhere. I have my truck and I can drive perfectly well."

"Joe, won't it be nice to have someone to do some cleaning and fixing you something to eat?" I asked.

"I guess it will be okay," he replied.

I knew I needed to bring up the issue of the gun. "I also need to make you are aware that Joe has a gun that he keeps beside his bed."

The woman perked up at that.

Joe quickly interjected, "I won't shoot anyone as long as they don't come in the house unannounced. And if they do, I won't shoot if they get on the floor."

I was impressed with how nonchalant the woman was as Joe talked about the gun. After discussing the cost and how services would be provided, she got up and walked toward the door. Joe stayed seated as we made our way out of the room. He seemed like he was more interested in what was on the television than what this woman had to say.

"Nice to meet you," he said as we exited the room.

We walked toward the door and I asked, "Can we talk a minute outside?"

Her car was parked at the end of the driveway. As soon as we were out of earshot, she looked at me and said, "Your father-in-law doesn't need to be left alone. We would like to help you but we can't send someone out unless the gun is removed from the house or locked up where he can't get to it."

"I totally agree with you. But I am not sure how we can force the help on him. Let us just try having someone come by a couple times a week. I will also make sure the gun is secured."

As the woman got in her car she stated, "Good luck and we will be in touch."

Walking back to the house, I thought we needed more than luck. We needed divine intervention.

It was determined that someone would come for five hours a day on Tuesdays and Thursdays. Mary Beth, Jay and I would rotate weekends until things changed.

On Wednesday, Dot from the agency came over to meet Joe. We sat on the back porch and looked out over the golf course while we all got to know each other. I was excited to learn that Dot had a strong personality and had also been in the military. I had a good feeling about this.

If I only knew...

Chapter 25

I will never leave you; never will I forsake you.
- Hebrews 13:5

The thought of leaving Joe alone was very difficult to consider but since he was determined to remain at 121 Hillshire Court, we had no option but to leave.

Thursday morning, Marilyn and I packed our bags before taking Joe to his last appointment. We had made a decision to leave as soon as we left the medical facility and had some breakfast together. It had been a long two weeks and we were ready to return to our homes and families.

Our last follow-up appointment was with the oncologist who was in charge of Joe's chemotherapy treatments who said, "I am amazed at how well you have tolerated both the chemo and the radiation. Many patients have to have a feeding tube inserted because of the effects of the radiation on the throat."

Throughout the entire six weeks, Joe rarely mentioned his throat being sore. The doctor then asked, "Do you have any other major concerns?"

I was waiting for this opportunity. "We have been seen by many different doctors in the last couple of months and no one seemed to care about Joe's dementia and how it was impacting his quality of life. We have been striving to make decisions that are best for Joe based not only on the prognosis of his cancer, but also his decline in cognitive abilities."

He seemed to truly understand my concerns. "I will write a note to tell my scheduler to make an appointment for an MRI. Hopefully it will be able to give you information that will help with his future treatment."

Once we got back to North Carolina, I had to follow up to make sure the MRI was being scheduled. When I finally got through to the scheduler, she told me the first available appointment was for November 3, an eternity away.

Chapter 26

*At midday you will grope around like a blind
person in the dark.*
- Deuteronomy 28:29

A cloud of confusion had begun to linger throughout Joe's days. He had no understanding of where he needed to be at any given time. We only received tidbits of information about what happened in the next couple of weeks. One thing was sure; even though Joe was four hours away, he was ever present in our thoughts and prayers.

Dot only came by a couple of times. Joe refused to let her drive him anywhere. The fourth scheduled time she was to come, Joe had gone somewhere, and after sitting in her car for almost two hours waiting for him, she left. The agency then called us to let us know that Joe wasn't at home. Jay called his father to check up on where he had been. The call only made Joe mad and he told Jay that it was none of his business.

The following morning, Joe had a dentist appointment. I called to remind him and he seemed to know exactly where he was going.

I received a call from the dentist's office to tell me that he didn't show up. I called Joe and he told me he went and they told him that he didn't have an appointment. I knew there was no need to argue.

The next morning around 8:30, Jay received a call from a doctor's office that Joe had never been to before. The receptionist told Jay that his father was standing in front of her. She informed Jay that Joe had never been to this office before and that he didn't have an appointment. This must have concerned her to the point of looking up contact information and calling Jay. After hanging up the phone Jay called his dad. "Dad, I just received a call from a doctor's office on Lake Murray Boulevard stating that you were just there."

Joe responded in an annoyed voice, "I thought I had an appointment."

"Dad, you have never been to that doctor's office before."

"Well, I am home now," Joe said as he hung up the phone.

Chapter 27

And the peace of God, which transcends all understanding,
will guard your hearts and your minds in Christ Jesus.
- Philippians 4:7

At this point, we were all extremely concerned about Joe
but didn't have any clear idea on how to proceed. Every day,
Jay and I would spend most of our time together discussing
different options. We knew that it would take a miracle from
God to persuade Joe that he needed to move to a place where
he could be closely monitored.

On Monday, September 22, Joe had a CT scan scheduled.
Mary Beth got in late Sunday night and woke up early to take
him to his appointment. She called me that morning while Joe
was at the doctor's office. Apparently, Joe had gone into the
kitchen to get something out of the refrigerator. As he reached
for the handle, he passed out, falling backwards and hitting the
back of his head on the floor. As Mary Beth reached for her
phone to call 911, Joe began to stir. The back of his head was
bleeding and he was truly shaken up.

Since Joe already had an appointment, Mary Beth decided to
take him and let the doctor know about the fall. After the scan
and a quick checkup, the doctor told them that the tumor from

the lung cancer had shrunk a little and that he was encouraged by what he saw.

The doctor also stated that he could not see anything from the tests to indicate a reason for Joe to lose consciousness. On the other hand, Joe was quite concerned about the fall and appeared ready to move to North Carolina. So after the appointment, they went back to Joe's house, packed his bag and left for Mary Beth's home in Greenville. When we heard the news, Jay and I were very excited that he realized that he shouldn't be left alone, but were unsure if living with Mary Beth would bring the peace we were seeking. Either way, we were encouraged by his change of mind.

There will always be differences of opinions in families. One member may believe that they know what is best while the others may not agree. This can cause a lot of strife in stressful situations if it is not handled with kid gloves.

Mary Beth had wanted Joe to move in with her ever since we began to realize that he would have to leave his home. She and her daughter lived in a two-bedroom apartment and had wanted to move into a bigger place. If Joe moved in, they would be able to afford a larger home and all could benefit from the arrangement.

Jay and I knew that Mary Beth was a wonderful caregiver. She had proven this when she took care of her mother. The major difference now was that she had to work and her daughter was an active teenager who needed a lot of her mother's time. We were also unsure that Joe would be content living in his daughter's house and not have his own space. This was one of those situations that had to play itself out. Again, I had to just believe that God is sovereign and in control of all circumstances, even this one.

Chapter 28

But as for me, I trust in you.
- Psalm 55:23

Sometimes, a higher power can direct our paths and open the doors needed for us to walk through. I can't help but think that this is exactly what happened during this extremely difficult time. I like to refer to this as our miracle.

After Mary Beth got back to Greenville, she called to discuss our next plan of action. She shared that Joe seemed antsy and just talked about going home. It just didn't seem like Joe would be happy living with either Mary Beth or us. This led us into conversing about having Joe placed in an assisted living community near his present home but then Mary Beth suggested that we look in New Bern, North Carolina. New Bern is a beautiful city nestled along the Neuse River. It is the home of our state's first capital and has many historic and nautical places to visit. Many years ago, Joe had thought about moving to this quaint town that was not far from the beach, a place he loved to visit.

As we were talking, I started searching for assisted living communities and was led to the website of Croatan Village. It is a small assisted living community right off of Highway 70, about thirty-five minutes from the coast. I called and was able to speak to the marketing director. I felt like God had led me to this site and immediately had a good feeling that this would be Joe's new home. It would be a two and a half hour drive for Jay and me and an hour drive for Mary Beth. If Joe would be willing to go and live there, it would be worth every minute of the drive.

On Thursday, Mary Beth drove Joe over to Croatan Village. They met with Lin, the marketing director, a wonderful person who sincerely cares about the residents and their families. She took Joe and Mary Beth around and introduced Joe to several war veterans. She showed them the units that were available and how the residents had decorated their space to make it feel like home. Joe appeared very happy during the time he was there and consented for us to investigate it further.

The next afternoon, I was walking my dog and thinking about Joe. I punched his number into my cell phone.

"Joe, how are you?"

"I am bored and tired of sitting in this room and watching television."

"How was your visit yesterday to Croatan Village?"

Joe spoke into the phone, "I don't remember going to New Bern and if we did go, we must have gone to the hardware store. By the way, I am ready to go home. I have places to go and need my truck."

I was in shock! Had he already forgotten his fall and why he was in Greenville with Mary Beth? My excitement left me like a helium balloon being busted. "Joe, don't you remember falling the other morning?"

"What fall?" he replied.

I knew that there was no way to get him to remember yesterday's events so I said goodbye and hung up the phone.

Mary Beth realized that her father was adamant about going home and felt there was no other option. So the next morning, Joe packed up his little suitcase and they drove back down to Columbia.

Chapter 29

For the Lord gives wisdom, and from his mouth come
knowledge and understanding.
- Proverbs 2:6

Was placing Joe into an assisted living community a broken promise? Clearly, Joe wanted to stay in his own home for the remainder of his life. Could things be different if he had kept his long-term health care policy active instead of discontinuing it a couple of years ago to save himself some money? Would our decision to move him been any different if Joe had had a closer relationship with his children? Is a feeling of guilt going to haunt us for the remainder of our lives because of the decisions we had made?

At this point we knew that we had to take action. The stress was just too much for all of us, and no matter how much Joe wanted to stay at home, it was no longer possible. Jay had the week off from work and we had a camping trip planned for the beach. This trip was a blessing and a time to get a plan of action into place. We love camping and enjoy getting away with our little home on wheels. That next morning, after spending the night at the campground I wrote in my journal:

Sitting on the beach. An absolutely beautiful day. It is hard to believe that it is close to eighty degrees on the last day of September. I had trouble sleeping last night. Thinking about the days to come. I have to realize that God doesn't exist in the worry. It is nice to have some peace. No one has trained us on how to do this. Dear Lord, give us wisdom.

After writing, we took a long walk on the beach and then called Croatan Village to see if we could go over and visit. Lin consented to meet us near the campground to discuss information regarding Joe and this move.

Jay and I met Lin at a McDonalds around 4:30 that afternoon. We instantly liked her and felt even better about our decision of moving Joe to New Bern. Lin shared some information and gave us a notebook full of paperwork to complete. We were glad to do whatever we needed to move Joe as quickly as possible. Since Jay was off this week, we planned on traveling to Columbia on Friday and moving him over the weekend.

I didn't realize what a miracle all this was until talking with several people who investigated assisted living communities for months and had to be put on waiting lists before an opening occurred. I truly believe God was intervening on Joe's behalf.

Chapter 30

Do not be anxious about anything, but in everything, by prayer and petition, with thanksgiving, present your requests to God.
- Philippians 4:6

On Wednesday morning, we awoke to birds chirping and a blue sky waiting for us as we opened our camper door. We began our morning with a fresh breakfast of eggs, bacon, and toast cooked on the outside grill. I have come to believe that whatever we fix, it just tastes better when cooked outside.

After cleaning up the dishes, we began breaking down the campsite. I typically spend my time wiping down everything inside the camper and packing the clothes while Jay does all the necessary stuff like flushing out the water lines and hooking the camper to the truck. Bee assists by sniffing around the campsite and barking at people and dogs that walk past. After checking out and turning in our keys, we made our hour trip to New Bern.

We were both getting a little bit anxious about this drastic move but knew deep down that we were making the right decision. Croatan Village is located on a side street right off Route 70 and ten minutes from the historic district.

After parking the camper and making sure Bee was secured, we made our way to the entrance. When we walked through the sliding glass door, we were greeted by a group of older men that were sitting in the lobby with huge grins on their faces. The receptionist smiled brightly as we introduced ourselves. Immediately, we both had a good feeling about this place that may be Joe's new home.

A couple of minutes after we entered the lobby, Lin appeared from behind the corner. She ushered us into her brightly lit office. "Please take a seat."

We sat down and couldn't help but notice the beach décor that she used to adorn her small space. "Joe will love your office. He has decorated his entire house with a nautical theme," Jay shared.

"I am very excited about Joe joining us. We enjoyed meeting him last week."

"Please pray that we will be able to convince him to come," I stated.

"Well, it is too bad that he won't be here for the next Romeo Club meeting at the Sanitary Fish Market."

Jay asked, "What is the Romeo Club?"

Lin responded with a smile, "The Romeo Club stands for retired old men eating out."

I knew that Joe loved hanging out with retired veterans and sharing his own war stories. He also enjoys the Sanitary Fish Market, a famous restaurant right on the water. He has made many trips down to Morehead City just to eat the blues, his favorite fish.

I asked, "When is it?"

"They are meeting this coming Monday morning."

Jay spoke up, "What time would we need to have him here?"

Lin replied, "The van leaves around 9:00."

I exclaimed, "We will be here! This will be a great incentive to get him to come. Also, I need to tell you that we can't stay very long today. We have our dog, Bee, in the truck."

Lin smiled at us, "Go get her. We allow dogs to come visit as long as they have their shots."

"Thanks, I will be right back." I ran back to the truck and clearly Bee was glad to see me.

When I reentered the building, Jay and Lin were finishing up on the paperwork. "Come on, I will show you Joe's unit."

Each unit had a large family room/kitchenette, bedroom, and a large bathroom. Everywhere we went appeared clean and lacked any type of unpleasant smell. Lastly, we walked by the dining room where lunch was being served. To my amazement, the food looked delicious and everyone looked very happy.

As we left that Wednesday afternoon, I believed in my heart that this was where Joe needed to be. Now the hard work was ahead of us. Jay and I were very excited but knew that we couldn't expect this to be an easy transition for Joe. Would he agree to come or would he dig in his heels and refuse to leave his home? Time would only tell.

Chapter 31

But those who plan what is good find love and faithfulness. -
Proverbs 14:22

I have learned from life that nothing comes easily and
we shouldn't expect this move to go ahead without major
obstacles. The first obstacle happened that Wednesday night.
I received a phone call from Karen. I told her we were going
to move Joe to Croatan Village this coming weekend. She
immediately responded that Joe was not going anywhere.
Apparently Joe had gone over to her house and told her that he
thought we were thinking about moving him and he was pretty
upset about it.

I was having a hard time believing what this woman was
telling me. Just like when we sat in Argene's memorial service,
I had to question who I was and what right this person had in
telling me that Joe was not going to come with us.

Argene's service was one I will never forget. I don't think
anyone could. A couple of years before the stroke, Argene
befriended a woman that happened to be one of Jay's former
girlfriends from Eastern North Carolina. She had moved to
Columbia with her husband and five children. Because of their
renewed friendship, it only made sense to invite her to the
memorial service.

Since Argene had not been an active member of a church at the time, Joe found a minister that was a friend of a friend. He came over the day before the service and we were able to share how we wanted the service to be conducted. I had recently gone to a memorial where people could get up and share a few words about the deceased. Given that the minister didn't know Argene, we thought filling time with some kind words from friends and family members would be a good idea.

An hour before the service was to begin, Cindy, Jay's former girlfriend, showed up at the house. She stated that she had been out and needed a place to change her clothes before going to the church. We thought this was kind of strange but went with it. When we arrived at the church, all the family members went to the front of the church to sit. The small church was filled with friends Argene and Joe had made since they had moved to Columbia.

The minister got up and began to speak. "We are here to remember Arlene Darrah."

Jay and I looked at each other. Did we hear that correctly? Sure enough he continued to address Argene as Arlene. At that point I thought the service couldn't go more astray than a misread name, but was I ever wrong.

Once the minister finished his short eulogy, he asked if anyone would like to speak. What a mistake that was! It was like Cindy had planned this moment for years. She walked up and got behind the pulpit and began to speak. She spoke about how the Darrah family was very special to her and even described past experiences with Jay when they were dating. She shared how she felt a bond with Argene and Joe that could never be broken.

After about five minutes, I began to question if I was Jay's wife or if she was. I also could tell that Jay was becoming more and more upset by her presence. Finally, after about ten minutes, the minister went over and placed his arm on Cindy's shoulder and told her it was time for her to sit down.

But Cindy just didn't know when to stop. When we went back to the house on Hillshire Court, she showed up. She spent a lot of time trying to talk with Jay but he wasn't having anything to do with her. Her husband came by an hour later to pick her up. It was clear to see that he was embarrassed by her behavior. Even then, she didn't want to leave.

To this day, I truly believed she wanted to go back to her childhood and be with the Darrah family instead of going home to her five children. It was a very sad sight. A couple of days later, Jay received a call from her. Still, she was trying to befriend him. After I spoke to her on the phone and told her how happy we were, she finally stopped contacting him.

So, just like Cindy, I felt Karen was acting like she was a member of this family and going to dictate what Joe was going to do. I assured her that Joe would be moving and to please step aside if she was not going to support our decision.

Jay and I discussed the need for a plan that could help Joe understand that staying in his home was not an option. As a special educator, I couldn't help but think about what worked best for children with autism or Asperger Syndrome. If you write down facts in a large format so it can be easily read, the children usually responds much better than trying to just tell them something. So that morning I spent about two hours writing down dates and incidents that had occurred over the last six months regarding Joe. I included the times we had driven down to see him, the missed appointments, the confusion in taking his medication, and how his general practitioner had told him that he had no business living on his own.

I showed the document to Jay and asked if he would allow

me to talk with his father. We had become more and more aware of how hostile Joe had become toward Jay in the last couple of weeks. We agreed that Joe would be more receptive if I took the lead in this endeavor.

Chapter 32

Love the Lord your God with all your heart and with all your
soul and with all your strength and with all your mind; and,
Love your neighbor as yourself.
- Luke 10:27

Both Jay and I tossed and turned the night before leaving
for Columbia. Traveling down the road, my heart felt like it
was going to come out of my chest. This entire situation was
beginning to affect us emotionally and physically. We did
listen to an incredible message by a guest speaker at Elevation
Church. One excellent point that I need to hold onto is that
God is good at being God. I need to remember that I am not in
charge of this situation but our gracious God is.

When we arrived, Joe was walking toward his backyard and
seemed a little confused when he saw us. He looked like he
was trying to find something and didn't acknowledge us. Both
Jay and I were anxious to have this conversation, so we went
inside and waited for him. Those couple of minutes seemed to
last forever. What if Joe refused to go to New Bern? Could we
force him? If he doesn't go, do we just get back in the truck
and go home?

When you enter Joe's house, there is a little dining room
to the right where he has his bills and miscellaneous papers

spread out on the table. We sat down there and waited. Jay and I were discussing how we would approach this intense conversation. I pulled out the paper that I had created and was reviewing it when we heard the door open. I immediately noticed Joe's defensive posture as he came in and faced us.

All I can remember is how nervous I was. I took a deep breath and asked, "Joe, can you come and sit down next to me? We would like to talk with you."

In a gruff voice he responded, "If you are going to talk with me about moving then I want to tell you right now, I am not going anywhere!"

"Can you please at least listen to what we need to say?" I asked in a pleading voice.

Thankfully, Joe sat down and looked toward the piece of paper. I read through the three pages of documentation beginning with his diagnosis of lung cancer and his doctor's concerns. As I went through the many events that led to this moment, I could tell he was beginning to understand why we were so adamant about this move. When I finished, I asked, "Joe, we are here to move you to Croatan Village. Would you please make this move?"

With his head down and in a very quiet voice, he said the words we had been praying for. "Yes, I will go."

I almost fell out of my chair as I reached over and gave Joe a big hug. Before we knew it, all three of us were crying and Jay and I were beaming at each other.

Chapter 33

Consider it pure joy, my brothers and sister whenever you
face trials of many kinds.
- James 1:2

I remember the next couple of hours almost like a dream.
I felt like I was holding my breath, afraid to say anything in
fear that Joe would change his mind and send us home. I have
heard that people pray more when they are desperate and I was
desperate. Many prayers were being lifted up in hope that Joe
would continue to cooperate with the move.

As soon as we got an affirmative answer, we went into high
gear. We had made a list of things we needed to do in order to
have Joe packed up and on the road to New Bern by Sunday.
Before Joe could change his mind, we placed him in the truck
and headed over to the local U-Haul store to pick up a trailer.

After attaching the trailer to the truck, we went to Joe's
favorite restaurant and had lunch. It was hard to find
conversations that wouldn't focus too much on what we were
doing. Neither Jay nor I wanted to bring up a topic that would
get Joe to think about his decision and possibly change his
mind.

While we were waiting for our food, I went outside to call

Mary Beth. "I wanted to let you know that Joe has agreed to move."

At first I didn't hear anything. "Mary Beth, are you there?"

"Yes," she said between sobs. "You have no idea how upset I have been. I couldn't help but think he wasn't going to leave."

"I know exactly how you are feeling. It is like a huge burden has been lifted."

"I will drive down tomorrow to help move him."

"That will be great. I think we are going to need as much help as we can get," I said. "We will keep you informed if anything changes. See you tomorrow."

When we got back to the house, we began the task of choosing the major items that Joe would take with him and what would later be distributed among family members. We tried to keep Joe busy sorting through items and kept the conversation to a minimum.

The neighbors realized what was happening when they saw the U-Haul backed up into the driveway and they started streaming through. Most of his neighbors were women close to his age. For years, Joe had been a fixture in their lives. Whenever something broke, he was called to repair it. Every spring, Joe tilled up the soil in a garden plot and grew fresh vegetables that he loved to share. On any given day, the neighbors would see Joe out in his yard and stop for a chat. Even though he had been experiencing some major cognitive changes, his neighbors and close friends still cared deeply for him. So it wasn't surprising to see the number of people come by to say goodbye and wish him well.

Chapter 34

Where you go, I will go and where you stay, I will stay.
- Ruth 1:16

Naomi must have had tremendous trust in Ruth's God as she told her that she was going to leave everything she ever knew and go with her to Bethlehem. Naomi only knew that Ruth had great faith and she desired to be around this woman for the remainder of her life. Jay and I also had to demonstrate faith that God would provide for Joe as we continued to pack up all his belongings and take him far from this place he had called home.

Later that night, after people had stopped coming in and we were watching a little television, I noticed Joe was getting very antsy. Jay had gone to bed and we were sitting alone in the living room. It was then that Joe spoke up.

"Cora, I can't do this. I appreciate everything you and Jay are doing but I need to stay here." There was a deep sense of anxiety sketched across his face that tore at my heart. It would have been so easy to comply with his wishes and walk away but I knew I had to be firm and demonstrate my faith that this was what was best.

I reminded Joe of the trip to the Sanitary Fish Market on

Monday with the Romeo Club. I also had to firmly tell him that it was what was best for him. It was very sad to see this man, who stood so proud for so many years, crumble before my eyes.

That night, before I closed my eyes, I thought about the battles that were won that day, and thanked God for being such a good God.

Chapter 35

Listen, my sons, to a father's instruction; pay attention and gain understanding.
- Proverbs 4:1

There comes a time, if a parent lives long enough, that the father-child relationship will reverse. A child looks up to his father throughout their early years and into adulthood. As the adult child matures and experiences life, they begin to see the relationship in a totally different light and either the ties will grow tighter or loosen up. Jay had always given his father respect but didn't agree with how he had been living his life over the last ten years. In the last nine months, Jay had to slide into the role of the guardian with all its responsibilities. It felt uncomfortable but everyone knew it had to be done.

The next morning, Joe got up and told us that he was ready to move. He began helping Jay move some of the furniture out to the U-Haul. It was clear that Joe's health was being compromised by the lung cancer. He was taking lots of breaks and didn't have the energy to pick up big items. He also had difficulty deciding on what items to keep and what to leave for us.

When Argene had died, Joe transformed his house into his own nautical paradise. Instead of moving to the beach, he brought the beach to him. Everything he had in his living room was nautical. The palm tree lamp and birds perched on poles were just a few unique items. All the pictures on the wall were of boats, beach scenes, or favorite coastal restaurants.

As we watched Joe choose the items he would take with him, it was the things he didn't choose that stood out to us. Years ago, Mary Beth and Jay had bought a really nice picture of a boat for him. We truly thought he liked it because of where it was hung. I had to laugh when I went into the room and all the pictures were taken off the wall except this one. Joe had also cleared off the items that were on top of the console. Everything was packed to go except a picture of Jay, Joe and I at the Hoover Dam. We just had to laugh and move on.

Mary Beth showed up and immediately began hauling items out to the trailer. Everyone worked with an extra spark of energy to move things out and make sure Joe would not attempt to stop the process and bring the move to a halt. We packed everything Joe would need for his new home except for his bed. That would be put in the trailer tomorrow before we pulled out.

While we worked, friends continued coming by the house to say their goodbyes, which caused some anxiety for Joe. It was clear that he was confused and several times didn't seem to understand that he was actually leaving. One of us had to be near to make sure the conversations didn't cause more stress than necessary.

After an exhausting day, we went out to a steak restaurant for dinner. Jay, Mary Beth, Joe and I piled into a booth and shared memories about the time at 121 Hillshire Court. We talked about the many friends Joe had made and the many handyman jobs he had completed over the years. Our conversation moved into a discussion about all we had accomplished so far but didn't discuss tomorrow and how Joe's world would be forever changed.

The people sitting at this table really are my family. We had gone through life together for over thirty-five years and we were closer than we had ever been. Even though the tension between Jay and Joe was not totally gone, it had definitely lessened over the last couple of days. The roles had definitely changed in the brief time we had been there and now Joe would need to rely on Jay more than ever before.

Chapter 36

*Commit to the Lord whatever you do, and your
plans will succeed.*
- Proverbs 16:3

Sunday morning was a beautiful day. Everyone got up early
and continued to pack up the U-Haul and other vehicles. We
had decided to drive up to New Bern later that afternoon so that
we could be at Croatan Village Monday morning in time for
Joe's trip with the Romeo Club.

Several of Joe's neighbors came by and sat on the back porch
and reminisced about all the years they had been neighbors. It
was a touching moment to watch Joe with his cronies, smiling
and sharing stories.

Our plan was to leave around 11:00 before Joe had too much
time to ponder his situation. We knew that no matter what time
we left it would be difficult, but we also knew that people with
dementia tend to struggle with confusion in the latter part of
the day and mornings tend to be the best time to make major
changes.

We were working at a brisk pace when Judy showed up. For
the last nine months, I had only seen Judy once. She had come

over one afternoon before one of Joe's chemo treatments. The two of them were sitting on the couch cuddling and making small conversation. Judy asked, "Cora, where does Joe go for his chemo treatments?"

"He is receiving treatment at South Carolina Oncology Associates which is right off Highway 20. I know Joe would love it if you could come by and sit with him. The chemo takes about four hours and I am sure he would appreciate your company."

For a second there, I really thought she might go. But needless to say, she never did.

So, around 10:30, Judy pulled up in her car and noticed the U-Haul in the driveway full of Joe's furniture. Not understanding what was going on, she ran into the kitchen with a frightened expression on her face. Mary Beth and I were sitting at the kitchen table talking and as I looked up I could tell that Judy was very disturbed.

She sat down and started crying. Through her tears she tells us, "Joe told me that he was only going to visit a place nearby. I told him earlier on the phone that I would go with him. He never told me that he was actually leaving."

"Judy, Joe is leaving today for North Carolina. Recently, he fell and he has not been taking his medication properly. He has been showing more signs of dementia and needs to be somewhere he can receive assistance." I wanted to tell her that if she had been around more, she would understand why we were making this move but I didn't want to cause any more strife.

Judy then looked right at us and declared, "You are taking my best friend away from me!"

There were so many things I wanted to say in response,

to this but instead I just looked at her with a sympathetic expression. I can't help but think that if this is how you treat your best friend, I'd hate to be just a friend. Anyway, enough about that.

Finally, Judy got herself together and walked out to where Joe was sitting. They began to hug and kiss each other. It was then that I knew that it was going to be a lot harder getting him into the car. Finally, around noon, after placing the last items into the truck, Judy realized that Joe was actually going to leave. So with tears and lots of kisses, she got into her own car and left.

The plan was for Joe to ride with Mary Beth in her car and Jay and I would follow with the truck and trailer. As we all got in our vehicles to leave, Joe continued to walk around his yard in disbelief. I can't imagine how difficult this was for him. All the fresh memories and ones lived over three decades clinging to him like a vine on a tree. When it became apparent that he would not get in the car, Jay got out of the truck and walked over to his dad.

"Dad, it is time to go. You need to get in the car with Mary Beth."

"No, I don't want to. I have changed my mind. I want to stay here."

"Dad, you can't. Mary Beth is waiting for you. We need to go now. All of your stuff is packed and we need for you to get in the car."

As Jay looked inside the car, he could see tears falling down Mary Beth's face. "Come on Dad," she said. "It will be all right."

Slowly, Joe slid into the passenger seat and Jay closed the door. Before he could say anything else, Mary Beth put the car in drive and our little caravan moved out of sight of everything Joe loved and cherished.

My heart truly hurt that day. I had no understanding how Joe must have felt leaving everyone he cared about to go to a *home* where he would lose many of the freedoms that gave him so much joy. My only prayer was that he could find some joy in his new life and come to appreciate his family that he had been separated from for so many years.

Chapter 37

The righteous person may have many troubles, but the Lord delivers him from them all.
- Psalm 34:19

As we started down the road, I was filled with so many emotions. I felt remorse for Joe, but I was primarily filled with an incredible sense of gratitude toward God. Only He could have changed Joe's mind and allowed the events to unfold in the manner that they did. All of us were extremely exhausted both mentally and physically. Even so, we knew we had to continue to move ahead toward New Bern and a new life for Joe.

We stopped for lunch at a fast food restaurant about an hour down the road. Jay ordered the food for us and all four of us gathered around a small table in the back of the restaurant.

"Where are we going?" Joe asked with a confused tone in his voice.

Mary Beth immediately answered, "Dad, don't you remember? We are going to New Bern to your new home."

Joe quietly responded, "Oh."

"Remember, tomorrow you are going to the Sanitary Fish

Market where you are going to hang out with the Romeo Club and eat some blues," Mary Beth stated with the hope that this might distract him from his difficult departure.

Joe seemed content with her explanation and exchanged small talk with us as we ate our food. Due to symptoms of his dementia, South Carolina was now all in the past. All Joe had left to hang on to was each present moment.

Jay and I headed to New Bern with the U-Haul trailing behind us while Mary Beth and Joe went back to Greenville to sleep at her house. The plan was that everyone was going to meet at Croatan Village around 9:00 AM the following morning in time for Joe to get on the van with the other members of the Romeo Club.

We checked into our hotel around 6:00 and I walked next door to the Golden Corral and fixed two takeout plates. Jay could hardly finish his food before he put his head down on the pillow and fell into a deep sleep. As Jay lay beside me, I pressed the numbers on my telephone and waited for Mary Beth to answer. "Hello."

"Hello, Mary Beth. I was checking to see how Joe is doing."

"He seems a little confused and anxious. I gave him an Ambien and he just laid down."

"Do you think he will be okay with this move?"

"I think he will be," she spoke in a tired voice.

"I am sure it will take some time for him to adjust, but it is for the best for him and all of us. I hope all goes well for the rest of your evening and we will see you in the morning." I placed the phone back on the bedside table and reached for my journal. After writing down the highlights of the day, I closed it and was soon fast asleep.

Chapter 38

A man's steps are directed by the Lord. How then can anyone understand his own way?
- Proverbs 20:24

What is a home? I have thought about this often in the last couple of weeks as we have made this transition for Joe. Since Argene died, he had transformed their home into a man cave filled with items that reflected his personal taste. He had a lot of pride in each distinct piece of furniture and every picture that hung on the walls. It was his security blanket and his refuge from the outside world. I can't begin to understand how he felt to be taken away from everything he knew and loved and be told that he will never go back. My prayer is for this place to somehow become home for him. Time will only tell.

Jay and I were up and ready to go around 8:00 the next morning. Before leaving the hotel, we took advantage of the breakfast bar down in the lobby. We just sat to eat when Jay's phone rang. "Mary Beth, what's up?"

"I just wanted to let you know that Daddy fell this morning in the bathroom. He hurt his elbow but he seems to be okay. I think he is pretty anxious about this move."

"Do you think he will be able to go on the trip to Morehead this morning?" Jay asked.

"Oh yes. We are on our way now. We will see you in just a couple of minutes."

Everything was actually becoming real. As we drove the truck up into the parking lot with all of Joe's belongings, a sense of peace fell over us. The grounds were set back from the main road by a large strand of pine trees. In front of the large one-story building was a pond that had a waterfall in the center. Several ducks were flapping their wings as they dove into the water for their morning bath. A small gazebo was to the left of the pond and close to the entrance of the building. As we made our way toward the front porch, several residents sat chatting in chairs that were lined up against the outside wall.

When entering the building, there are two offices to the right and a spacious lobby on the left. On that fall day, the office doors and coffee tables were decorated with colorful autumn arrangements. There was a table set up against a wall with a huge container of fresh lemonade. On the opposite side of the lobby was a table with festive decorations and a visitor's sign-in book. Once you pass through the lobby, there are two long hallways to the left and right with the dining room straight ahead.

Joe's unit was located at the end of the hallway to the right. As we made our way toward our destination, we passed a brightly lit library with a table set up in the center for a puzzle. After the library, decorated doors with elaborate fall wreaths paved the way to the unit that would now be Joe's new home.

Lin met us with a key to open the outside door at the end of the hallway so that we could easily transport Joe's furniture into his space. A middle aged man came down the hall with a cart for us to use. Just about this time, Mary Beth and Joe pulled up in her car. Joe immediately came over and began pulling items out of Jay's truck.

Jay addressed me concerning his father. "Cora, can you please have Dad stay in the room so he won't fall again?"

"I will try but he seems pretty determined to help."

Just about that time, Lin walked up to Joe. "Joe, let's go. The van is here to take us to Morehead."

Mary Beth turned toward her father. "Come on Dad, I will walk with you."

Lin and Mary Beth led Joe over to the white van that had Croatan Village painted on the side. It was clear from watching him that he seemed to want to stay and help us unpack. But with the support of both Lin and Mary Beth, he climbed up the steps into the van.

While Joe was away, we were able to unload all his furniture and personal items. We decorated the room to imitate his home back in South Carolina as closely as possible. As we were finding places for the last of his personal items and making up his bed, Joe and Lin returned and could be heard walking down the hall.

Once they entered the room, Lin exclaimed, "Joe, this is such a cool room. I love the palm tree light and your collection of beach pictures. It is clear that we both love the beach."

Joe found his way to his red leather couch and sat down. From the smile on his face, he seemed to be pleased with how the rooms turned out. "How did all this stuff get here?"

I chimed in, "Joe, don't you remember, we drove it down in the U-Haul and Jay's truck?"

"It sure does look nice," Joe said as he gazed around the room.

After Lin left, we gave Joe a tour of his room and where all of his clothing, toiletry items, and valuables were kept. We chatted for a little while longer, and then prepared to leave. Once again, Joe reached out to hug his daughter and me and only extended his hand to Jay. I still had faith that one day hugs would be exchanged between these two men and they could actually demonstrate how much they cared about each other.

Chapter 39

People have heard my groaning, but there is no
one to comfort me.
- Lamentations 1:21

I once heard that God demonstrates his love by not allowing us to see into the future. As I reflect back on the past year, I am grateful for not knowing the future. I am sure it would have made it even harder than it was.

The first week or so, we didn't hear from Joe except with a quick phone call. We thought we might hear from someone at Croatan but have since learned that assisted living communities don't infringe upon their residents unless there is an emergency. Joe has a flip phone that apparently has been misplaced on a couple of occasions since he moved in. Once, when we asked why he hadn't picked up his phone, he told us that someone had come into his room in the middle of the night and stolen both his phone and his charger and then the next night returned the phone but not the charger. After a brief search, his charger was found on the table.

On October 19, Jay and I drove down to New Bern for the first time since we moved him in on the 6. It was a beautiful Sunday when we arrived at Croatan Village. As we turned the corner to his hallway, Joe was sitting in a chair outside of his unit. The closer we got to him, we could see that he was looking through one of the books we had packed for him. Once he gazed up and saw that it was us, he began to smile.

At first, we thought he was going to share how happy he was but his smile quickly was replaced by a look of desperation. "Jay, please take me away from here! There is nothing to do and I want to go home. If you won't take me home, I want to go to your house and live in your camper. I won't be any trouble. I will only need to come in to use the bathroom."

I couldn't believe that this man who months ago couldn't sleep one night in the camper was now pleading to live in it. He reminded me of a small child begging a parent to let him out of his room after being punished.

We tried to distract him by taking him to lunch but he continued to plead with us. After several minutes of not responding to his pleas, I was almost ready to give in when he settled down and seemed to be resigned to his situation. We left the restaurant and found a park on the river where we went and sat on a bench close to the water. He pulled out a magazine that he had found at the restaurant and withdrew into his own thoughts. The chilly air clung to us as we sat quietly immersed in our thoughts. Jay got up to walk near the water while Joe read his magazine and I pondered over the many changes that had taken place. It was truly an enjoyable time listening to the water lap up on to the shore and watching the boats sail by. I will always remember this moment, suspended between what used to be and what is now.

Chapter 40

*In all your ways submit to him, and he will make
your paths straight.*
- Proverbs 3:6

Since moving Joe to New Bern, we now had to travel back
and forth to Columbia to get the house ready for sale. As I
reflect back on this entire process, I have to give God the
credit for placing just the right people in our path to allow us
to accomplish this goal. In mid-October, my daughter Sara and
I traveled down so that she could choose some items that she
may want for her house.

On the way, she suggested that I call a realtor and see if they
could meet with us the next day. I had my laptop with me and
found a Coldwell Banker office near the house on Hillshire
Court. As she drove, I called and was transferred to Charles
Sibley. We spoke for a few minutes and he told me that he and
his wife would come over and talk with us the next morning.

Once I met Charles and his wife Dianne, I knew instantly
that I wanted to work with them. Jay was happy for me to go
ahead with this process and make the decisions since I had the
flexibility to travel back and forth for the next couple of weeks.
So after meeting for about an hour, I signed the contract to
allow them to represent us. We walked through the house and

they made many suggestions on what needed to be done to get the house ready for the market. When we parted, they handed me a list of different service providers that I could call.

We knew that the carpets needed to be replaced and so I contacted a man named Bryan to come over and give me an estimate. I made plans to return the following Wednesday and meet with a home inspector, Bryan, and someone to spray for bugs.

Bryan arrived around 2:00 and we walked through the house measuring for carpet. As we went into each room, he noticed lots of work that needed to be done.

He asked, "Have you considered using a contractor? I have a good friend who does excellent work. He hasn't worked much in the last couple of months due to the death of his son. I believe this would be a perfect job for him and also help you out."

"Sure, go ahead and call him. If he can come today, that would be wonderful."

In less than an hour, Mike knocked on the door. After introductions, I gave him permission to look around. He walked through the house taking notes and looking for all possible problems that would need to be addressed. At this time, I was working with the home inspector and the guy taking care of the pest issue. After everyone had left, Mike shared with me the issues he thought he could handle for us. I immediately knew that Mike was someone who could manage this challenge and could also be trusted. So we arranged for him to draw up a proposal and we would confer in the next couple of days.

Now I know that some people would consider me naïve but I think of it as trusting God. From the moment that Mike took over, things began to roll. He was able to find an excellent painter to paint the entire house, a roofer to fix some major problems, a chimney sweep to clean out the birds that had been nesting in it for who knows how long, and a foundation company to fix a major issue in the rear of the house. And all the work was done in less than two months!

Mike was up front and expected quality workmanship from the people who completed the work at 121 Hillshire Court. He was constantly calling us with updates and charged us a reasonable amount for his labor.

I personally give God the credit for His intervention in one more facet of this journey. His presence has become so clear that when we discuss our situation, you can hear us say, "It's just a God thing."

Chapter 41

Therefore I tell you, do not worry about your life,
what you will eat or drink; or about your body,
what you will wear.
- Matthew 6:25

A couple of weeks before the move from Columbia, I had noted that Joe had lost his appetite and instead of eating a sensible portion of food, he only picked at it. This was a huge change from only a few of months ago when he was eating everything on his plate. One night, I cooked country-style steak and mashed potatoes, which was one of his favorites. I was surprised when Joe only had a couple of scoops of his mashed potatoes and only one bite of steak. This alarmed me because Joe had already lost a lot of weight from the cancer treatment and was becoming weaker.

Since he had been in New Bern, Joe was eating even less and losing more weight. We had conversed with the staff about how thin Joe had become and discussed options. They noted that Joe was choosing to stay in his room and miss meals. And if he did go, he ate very little. The staff had begun giving him a thick type of shake before every meal but most of the time Joe only took a sip or two.

The staff called on November 18 and expressed their

concerns about Joe's weight loss and his inability to make it down to the dining hall. They asked if Joe could be moved to a closer unit. We had already planned to visit on that day and were on the road when we received the call. When we arrived, the staff was in the middle of moving Joe. They had moved the big furniture but requested the family members move the personal items to their new destination.

Jay didn't find any humor in this move due to the amount of moving he was having to do down in South Carolina. Almost every other week, he was traveling down to the house on Hillshire Court to move more stuff out. The previous weekend, Jay had loaded up his truck with the last of the valuables and brought it to Durham where we had planned a yard sale. Mike had rented a dumpster and Jay and Mary Beth had literally filled it up with junk from Joe's workshop. So, moving anything, even just from down the hall was not what Jay had wanted to do while visiting his father. On the other hand, I personally thought it was very cool how it had been planned for the one day that we were coming to visit. This way we could make sure that his personal items were safely moved and pictures hung in just the right spots.

Our hope for Joe was that now that he was closer to the dining room he would make the short trip to eat his meals with the other residents. This could help him become stronger and more connected to others. But as we were learning from this roller coaster ride, we had no control over how Joe would respond to the external changes that were put into place.

Chapter 42

The Lord makes firm the steps of the one who delights in him; though he may stumble, he will not fall, for the Lord upholds him with His hand.
- Psalm 37:23-24

The next day, Marilyn flew into Durham to help us with the yard sale and be with Joe over Thanksgiving. Mary Beth drove in late Friday night to also help. That Saturday morning was very cold and not the best day for a yard sale. Earlier in the week, we had placed an ad on Craigslist with pictures of many of the tools that were for sale. Marilyn and I had baked treats and brewed coffee for all the brave souls that attended our yard sale on this brutal morning. Jay built a fire in a barrel and placed it close enough to feel the warmth as we sold our wares.

It was amazing the number of men that came out for the tools. After just a couple of hours, the big-priced items were gone and we crammed what was left into the truck to take to the Durham Rescue Mission. It ended up being a lot of fun talking with neighbors that we rarely see and standing around the fire conversing with friends and family.

The following Thursday, we all met at Croatan Village for our Thanksgiving meal. I had informed the staff that I wanted to reserve the private dining room for our family since it would be ten of us, including three small children. I told them that we would bring our own food if they could provide beverages for us. Jay received a call earlier in the week saying that all the food would be provided. This was a true blessing.

There are certain holidays that have been very special to me during my lifetime. As a child, Thanksgiving was always spent at a farmhouse in the country surrounded by my mother's family. We would typically arrive around noon and spend hours tramping through the woods down to the river that crossed the property. I can still hear the crunching of the leaves and the sound of rushing water over the assorted rocks that rose above the water line. My uncle had an old Jeep with only a roll bar to hold onto. All the children would take turns riding through the woods or down beaten dirt roads holding on as the Jeep popped up and down like a ride at the fair. The day would end with a huge feast of roasted turkey, sweet potato casserole, and all of the fixings.

Every Thanksgiving I ever had before my mom died was shared with her. That is why when she died in November, my perception of this holiday was forever transformed. From that point on, each year, we would change things up to bring life to this holiday that had somehow died with my mom's passing.

I will always have fond memories of that Thanksgiving Day at Croatan. As promised, a full course meal was waiting for us when we arrived. The private dining room was open and the table set for our family. There was turkey and ham and a large assortment of vegetables and desserts. Many of the employees stuck their heads in to make sure we had everything we needed. They truly made us feel at home.

The only downside to this day was Joe's health. It was clear that he had become weaker since the last time we saw him. He no longer chose to go out of the building and now he was rarely leaving his room. Jay had to walk beside him to make sure he didn't fall. Mary Beth had made him a plate of the food he usually loved to eat. After chewing only a couple of bites, he pushed the plate away.

Once everyone finished eating, we made our way back to Joe's room. But after only a couple of feet, he began to falter. Mary Beth found a chair and Joe sat down in the middle of the hall. This was a perfect moment to take pictures. All of us pulled out our cameras or cell phones and tried to create a permanent image of this little family that hardly knew each other just a couple of months ago.

After a couple of minutes, Joe was able to make it back to his unit. The kids took advantage of the nice weather and spent their time running around outside and peeking their heads in the window. The adults sat in Joe's small sitting room talking and laughing through the memories of this past year. Joe and Eli, my one-year-old grandson, had truly bonded. Eli was very content just standing near Joe, playing with his toys. Likewise, Joe seemed to enjoy the attention he was receiving from such a young child.

Chapter 43

But encourage one another daily as long
as it is called 'Today.'
- Hebrews 3:13

Over time, we had begun to notice a gradual change in
how Joe viewed the world. Instead of being angry about his
situation, he seemed to have taken on a grateful attitude that
suited him quite nicely. His smile brightened up the room when
we would come for a visit. He constantly thanked us for our
time and seemed genuinely grateful for anything we brought
him. Here was a man who previously didn't want to be near his
family and now seemed to really enjoy our company.

There were no more mentions of his life on Hillshire Court
or the many people he left behind. His memories seemed
to be predominantly of the life he had in New Jersey or in
the military. Because of this, we had several interesting
conversations pertaining to his time in the service. During one
visit, we primarily talked about his responsibilities as a load
master on a C-123 that he flew in over Vietnam.

These memories rise to the top because of the reminders that
have been placed in his new little home. Years ago, he attached
his important medals onto a piece of cardboard. Above all
the medals, he placed a set of wings that he was awarded in

Vietnam. There is a space between the wings and the other medals that he believes once held another set of wings. Every time we would come to visit, he would tell us that someone must have stolen the second set of wings. Since there is no need to argue with someone who has dementia, we began to expect the topic to always go back to the missing wings.

One day as Jay was looking through some of Joe's personal items, he found another set of wings and when Joe was not paying attention, he placed them under the first set of wings. Jay then propped the cardboard with the medals and wings in its usual place on the bookshelf and waited to see what Joe would say.

Joe sat down on his red couch and looked toward the bookshelf that held the piece of cardboard. "I think that second pair of wings is from China," he told us. "There should be a number on the back."

And then without missing a beat, he stated, "There should be a third set of wings somewhere. I believe someone must have stolen it."

Chapter 44

*The Lord himself goes before you and will be with you; he
will never leave you nor forsake you. Do not be afraid;
do not be discouraged.*
- Deuteronomy 31:8

I once had a hospice nurse tell me that people usually die
in much the same way they have lived their lives. Some die
quickly and quietly while others fight off death. I can tell Joe
is a fighter. He has fought us throughout this entire process and
he isn't finished fighting yet.

In early December, Joe's health took a turn for the worse.
He spent most of his days in the bed. Just getting up to use the
bathroom was becoming more and more difficult. Mary Beth,
Jay and I had been to see him and we were all very worried
about his rapid decline. While Jay was talking to his dad, Mary
Beth and I went down to the nurses' station to discuss our
concerns. Once we were there, I asked, "Can we speak with the
RN concerning Joe Darrah?"

"Wait right here while I get her." The nursing assistant
knocked on a door beside the station and the RN on duty
opened the door.

"Come in," she said as she motioned us to two chairs in front of her desk.

It was clear that Mary Beth was upset as she said, "We are very concerned about my dad, Joe Darrah."

"We also have been troubled about his health status," the RN stated. I could tell she was waiting for us to continue.

"What do we need to do to have hospice come in?" I asked.

"I will need to get an order from our physician assistant. She will be here in the next day or so. When she comes, I will have her visit Joe and write the order."

By this time, Mary Beth was wiping tears from her face. "Thank you," she stated in a muffled voice.

"Hospice will call you and set up an appointment to meet. Expect the call in the next few days."

As we went back to Joe's unit, Mary Beth continued to wipe tears from her face and tried to make herself look like she hadn't been crying.

Chapter 45

Don't be afraid, for I am with you.
- Isaiah 41:10

One Saturday night soon after hospice had been called in, Mary Beth went to visit her father. She noticed that he was in great pain and it looked like he may pass away that night. She called the hospice nurse to come over to assess him. A pain medication was prescribed and after taking it, Joe seemed better. The nurse told Mary Beth that we probably needed to go ahead and celebrate Christmas because he might not live but a few more days.

The thought of her father dying alone terrified Mary Beth. She had been with her mother for the many years that she had been in a comatose state, giving her excellent care. The weekend that her mother had passed away, she had gone back up to North Carolina and was not there when Argene took her final breath. I am not sure if this still haunts Mary Beth, but I do believe it played a part in the decision she made that day in December.

Mary Beth called Jay and told him that she was going to have her father moved to Greenville to stay through Christmas. She had called hospice and they had already delivered a hospital bed to her home. Jay didn't agree with this decision but Mary

Beth has dual power of attorney and had the right to move him. She had spoken to Joe about it and he seemed to have been in agreement.

The following day, my daughter and I arrived in New Bern to see Joe before he left. I walked into his room where he was sleeping.

"Joe, are you awake?"

He opened his eyes and reached for my hand and with the most desperate voice he pleaded to me, "Please let me stay here."

"Joe, this is not my decision. You need to speak with Mary Beth," I quietly said.

"I want to be here. If I have to get up in the middle of the night, I can call someone to help me."

"Joe, I will get Mary Beth and we can discuss it." I went into the adjacent room and motioned for Mary Beth to come hear what her father had to say.

"Mary Beth, I want to stay here. I am sorry if I caused you trouble but I want to be here in my own bed."

Mary Beth looked at her dad with compassion, "Dad, we talked about it yesterday. I have already gotten a hospital bed placed at my house. Don't you remember we talked about this?"

Joe seemed desperate when he replied, "Mary Beth, I will pay you back for any inconvenience, but I want to be here."

It was obvious that Mary Beth was upset and she walked out of the room, saying, "Okay, I will call hospice and have them come get the bed."

With relief streaming across his face, Joe whispered, "Thank you."

After I knew that Joe was okay, I went toward the lobby and saw Mary Beth sitting outside on the porch. I felt sad for her because I knew she only wanted what she thought was best for her father. I sat down beside her and placed my arm around her. "Mary Beth, I am sorry that it didn't work out the way you wanted."

"I just don't want him to die alone," she said through her tears.

"I know."

We sat there for a couple of minutes and then returned to see how Joe was doing. It was clear that he was feeling better now and we ended up having a nice visit.

It was amazing to think that just a couple of weeks ago, he insisted on leaving and now he seemed content to die in this place he now calls home.

We did go to visit Joe the Sunday before Christmas and celebrated our time together as a family. Mary Beth had gotten barbecue from one of our favorite restaurants and we brought sides and dessert for everyone. Joe sat on the couch while the rest of us sat at the table eating our Christmas meal. He wasn't hungry, but we tried to include him as much as possible. Many times, I would look over at him and he would just smile. It appeared that he sincerely was enjoying being with his family.

Chapter 46

But a Samaritan, as he traveled, came where the man was;
and when he saw him, he took pity on him.
- Luke 10:33

I recently heard a hospice nurse say, "A man is a man once and a child twice." This has become so true for Joe.

It is now mid-January and Joe continues to fight for another day. Life has become an extreme effort for him. Just getting up and going to the bathroom takes all the energy he can muster. He has been willing to let the nurse assistant come every Monday, Wednesday, and Friday to bathe him. The last time we visited, he asked if Rub-a-dub was coming. We looked at each with a puzzled expression. We asked him who Rub-a-dub was and he told us it was the little woman who comes and gives him a bath. I would love to give this woman a hug for providing this service to Joe in such a thoughtful manner that he would give her such an endearing name.

Our conversations have also taken on a certain pattern. He will usually start by asking about my family. I share a little about my daughter who lives with us and what dance or art projects she is working on. I then tell him about my other daughter who is a nurse, a mother of three, and expecting another baby. A couple of minutes will pass, and then he will ask again about my family. Then I will usually tell him again what I had just said only minutes before. I have learned in these last couple of months that there is no need to argue or tell him that he just asked me these questions. What is the point in it? Instead shouldn't we just be there for our loved ones as their minds fade and give them just a little self-dignity?

The literature that was given to us by hospice gives a sketchy outline of the process of death and the signs that most people exhibit in the last couple of months, weeks, and days. Food is not essential and should not be forced. There is a period of withdrawal that a person goes through. Sleep increases and there is less of a need to communicate. Inwardly, the person spends time processing their life. The person begins to slip between the physical and spiritual world. This is where I see Joe at this time.

My husband continues to have a difficult time forgiving Joe, but I truly believe he is coming around. No hugs have been exchanged but I pray that will happen before Joe slips away. I can't help but think about how great God has been to all of us throughout this last year. He has definitely carried us through extremely turbulent waters and is now bringing us to the shore.

Chapter 47

He went in and said to them, "Why all this commotion and wailing? The child is not dead but asleep."
- Mark 5:39

It has become clear in these last few weeks that Joe has begun to acknowledge the fact that he is dying. Pieces of his life have been stripped away and what held meaning no longer has value. This became crystal clear the day Joe handed over his beloved Rolex watch to Jay. It had become too heavy to wear and lacked the sentimental value that it once had.

Along with the watch, it was now time to have his personal bed replaced with a hospital bed. We arrived on a Monday morning and began by dismantling his bed while Joe sat on his couch in the sitting room. In times like these, it is wonderful when something humorous occurs to replace the awkward silence of the moment. As Jay took the headboard off and was walking by Joe in the sitting room, Joe began to wave to it like it was a dear old friend. "Goodbye, bed."

This one little action changed the entire mood of what was being done. Instead of feeling bad about taking Joe's bed away, he allowed us to complete this task with the knowledge that he knew it was for the best.

This man, who only months ago fought over discarded wood and finances, was now content with just being in bed sleeping or thinking about his life. It appears the bitterness and hardness that has surrounded his heart for so long has been replaced by a sense of contentment.

It was during this time that we had begun to take hold of the idea that Joe would only be getting worse. He hadn't been able to get out of bed or walk farther than his couch in weeks. Our minds had accepted the fact that we would probably be receiving a call from hospice to come and pay our last respects. So one afternoon when Mary Beth went to visit Joe, she was shocked when she found him hunched over his walker in the hallway outside the dining hall. She noticed that he was wearing a pair of brown shoes, pajama bottoms, and his t-shirt. When entering the building, she had to do a double take to comprehend what she was seeing. There was Joe, clutching on to his leather wallet with one hand and holding onto the walker with the other, scooting down the hall toward the dining room. "Dad, what are you doing out in the hall?"

Joe looked toward the closed dining room doors. "I'm going to the mess hall to buy me some food."

"Dad, the dining room is closed. Let's go back to your room and I will find you some food."

Joe obediently shuffled back to his room and sat down at the table to wait for his next meal.

Chapter 48

*I am not saying this because I am in need, for I have learned
to be content whatever the circumstances.*
- Philippians 4:11

It has been a couple of weeks since I last wrote in my
journal. Just as we thought the boat was coming ashore and
Joe would soon meet his maker, he has made an incredible
comeback. I am not sure exactly why his health has improved
but we are grateful for it. After talking with the personnel at
Croatan Village, we learned it could be something as simple
as a peanut butter and jelly sandwich. Joe will only eat what
he wants to at this time and to him, there is nothing as good as
peanut butter and jelly on white bread.

The next time Mary Beth visited her father, she found
him dressed in regular pants for the first time in months. His
waistline had shrunk and his pants appeared to be ready to
fall off but it was encouraging that he had made the effort
to put them on. They decided to take a walk down the long
hallway and she could hardly keep up with him as he pushed
his red walker farther down toward the nurse's station. Their
destination was the back hallway where the scale was located.

Mary Beth was not surprised when her father stood on the
scale and the number 117 appeared. Joe had lost close to thirty

pounds in the last three months. He didn't seem concerned as he stepped off the scale and took hold of his walker to make his way back to his room. They stopped on the way back and sat on a couch that someone had left in the hallway. People stopped to say hello and state that they were glad to see him out of his room. Joe returned the pleasantries and appeared to be truly content with his new life.

Chapter 49

*Trust in the LORD with all your heart; do not lean
on your own understanding.*
- Proverbs 3:5

Last night, Jay and I were discussing his father and his new recovery. Some of the old concerns about our decision to move his father were brought up. Did we do the right thing? Now that Joe is feeling better, could he have gone back home if we hadn't dispersed all of his personal belongings and put his house on the market? I wonder how many other family members struggle with this same thought once they have placed their loved ones in assisted living communities.

Even though Joe may have demonstrated signs of getting better physically, there was no indication that his dementia had gone away. He continued to live in a world of his own making that wasn't based on reality. From the conversations we have had in the last couple of months, Joe lives in a timeless state where he doesn't understand what day or hour it is. His only point of reference comes from when his tray arrives for him to eat. Even then, he isn't sure if it is time for lunch or dinner.

Joe has also begun hallucinating and has trouble knowing what is real and what isn't. The other day he told me that he had gone down to see his neighbor Don who lived up the street in Columbia. While he was there, a man showed up and told Don and Joe to begin using oxygen and that he would let them know when they could stop using it. Joe seemed distressed about always having to wear the oxygen. And even when he did wear it, it usually was on incorrectly. He told me he hoped the man would show up soon so he could take the tube out of his nose.

Even with the hallucinations and evidence that the dementia is still progressing, the question still haunts us. Could we have done something different to allow Joe the opportunity to stay in his own home? Could we have figured out how to have given him the kind of care he needed where he loved living? We can plague ourselves with these questions, but we also must face reality. It is now a moot point since the house has been cleaned out, improvements made, and placed on the sales market. Still our minds play havoc on us now that Joe's health seems to be improving. To make the situation even more confusing, Jay received a voice message from Joe this afternoon.

"Jay, can you come pick me up tomorrow and take me home? I have things that I need to do. Please call me back."

Now what do we do?

Chapter 50

The Lord is my portion; therefore, I will wait for him.
- Lamentations 3:24

What is a home? How would I feel if I was taken away from all that I knew and placed in a foreign environment? I have lived in the same house for the last thirty-one years. I have driven down the same streets and walked the same neighborhoods. I greet the same neighbors and travel to the same stores, visit the same church, and most of all, live within the same walls.

My home is where I feel safe and protected. I have control over this environment and can decide when to go to sleep and what to eat for dinner. I can watch TV or listen to any type of music that I want.

For many like Joe, this has been taken away. The elderly end up in assisted living communities, nursing homes, and memory care units. They are given as much independence as possible but still their world has been shrunk to the restraints of the building and grounds that they reside in.

For Joe, his life is lived within the confines of his two rooms. Either lying in bed or sitting on his red leather couch watching TV. Now that he has obtained more energy, his world has expanded to the hallways and the dining room. He has also begun to keep his door open so that he can greet the other inhabitants of this community.

Today Mary Beth called to tell us about her visit to see Joe. When she arrived, he was in the dining room eating dinner like he had been there every day since he arrived. She noticed that he had eaten most of his meal and was enjoying the company of the three men assigned to his table.

This major recovery has led to a new question. Will hospice pull back services? Mary Beth called hospice and spoke to the nurse in charge of Joe's care. She told her that Joe's lungs are sounding worse, not better. Because of this, hospice will continue.

Chapter 51

*Blessed are the peacemakers, for they will be
called children of God.*
- Matthew 5:9

It has been two weeks since we last saw Joe. We had heard that he had been doing better, but were able to see it with our own eyes. Physically, he has definitely improved. He was wearing the blue collared shirt that he wore the first couple of days he came to his new home. He had just returned from the dining room when we entered. We stopped at Wendy's to buy him a cheeseburger and offered it to him. He stated that he wasn't hungry and thought he had been to the mess hall for lunch. Jay had purchased Joe a pair of skinny jeans and he went into his room and changed his pants. A month earlier, this would have taken too much energy. Now, he was winded but seemed excited about his new pants.

We noticed that he was out of drinks and asked if he wanted to go with us to purchase a couple items. He eagerly arose from the red sofa, took his oxygen off and headed for the door. He wanted to leave his walker behind but Jay wasn't sure if he could walk to the truck without it.

I went to the nurses' station to sign him out. It had been almost three months since he left these walls. We are still so perplexed by what had happened to Joe to make him so sick to the point of death. And now we are just as puzzled by his dramatic recovery. As I signed him out, the nurse shared with me how wonderful it has been to see Joe up and around.

As we drove the couple miles down the road to the Dollar General, Joe stared out the window. He only made small talk but truly seemed happy to be out and about. We only stayed out for about thirty minutes before making our way back to his residence. As we pulled under the breezeway, he looked at Jay and asked, "Is this my home?"

"Yes, Dad."

Joe just shook his head and waited for us to open his door so he could get out.

It was clear that the little outing had taken a lot out of Joe but he truly seemed to appreciate it. Once we entered his unit, he sat down on the couch and stared at his medals that sat on the cardboard on top of the bookcase. Then, like a recording he stated, "You know, there should be three sets of wings but someone has taken one of them."

"Do you want us to look for the third pair of wings?" I asked.

"No, that's okay. Last night I went to the store that is at the end of the building. I had to walk under a barbed wire fence to get to it. I went to see if they had a pair of wings that I could buy."

"Oh, really," Jay said nonchalantly.

When it was time to go, Joe, wearing his skinny jeans, walked us to the front door. And as always, he shook Jay's hand and reached over to give me a hug.

Chapter 52

*So when you give to the needy, do not
announce it with trumpets.*
- Matthew 6:2

Good news! We have an offer on the house at 121 Hillshire Court. The buyers asked for $3,000 less than we were offering and we accepted. This now means only a couple of trips back down to South Carolina to pick up the furniture we left for staging and to clean out the shed.

Yesterday, Jay and I decided to go in two different directions. He went to Columbia and I to New Bern. Our new puppy continues to wake up around 4:45 and has been serving as our alarm clock for the last six weeks since he has been with us, joining Bee in our household of French Bulldogs. So, like many mornings, we got up early and prepared for our journeys. Jay left first due to his four-hour drive and was about an hour away from his destination by the time I got on the road.

I knew that the trip would probably cause my leg to ache so I decided to stop about midway and purchase a couple of items for Joe. He loved the skinny jeans we bought him so I stopped to purchase another pair of jeans and buy him some more Pepsi Colas. I didn't realize until driving by the *Welcome to New Bern* sign that this was the birthplace for Pepsi. I had to smile at thinking that Joe never used to care for this soft drink, but since being here, he can't get enough of it.

When I arrived around 10:40, Joe was still in bed. He gazed up at me and a smile began to form across his unshaven face. "Pull up a chair and visit for a while."

"Why are you still in the bed?" I asked.

"There isn't anything to do around here."

"Well, I am here to take you out to lunch."

"I am not feeling like it today, Shug, but we can eat in the mess hall." It always amused me when he referred to the dining room as the mess hall. I wondered if his mind had taken him back to the days when he was in the service.

We had about thirty minutes before lunch so we sat on the red couch and talked. Mae from across the hall saw that Joe was up and came in to say hello. I knew she attended the church service on Sundays and hoped that Joe would be motivated to join her so I asked, "Mae, tell me about the church service they have here at Croatan Village."

"It starts around 9:30 and the preacher is really nice."

I chimed in, "Joe, why don't you consider going to church tomorrow?"

He didn't appear to be interested and just replied, "9:30 is just too early."

I whispered to Mae, "If you see that he is up, please ask him if he will join you in the morning."

"I will be glad to," she whispered back as she slowly walked out the door.

Joe and I made our way toward the dining hall. A crowd had already started to gather around the door. Many in wheelchairs waited patiently for the doors to open. Others in walkers smiled shyly at us as we drew near.

Is this what getting old is like? Waiting for the doors to open to the dining hall? There were very few conversations, just people quietly waiting. I noticed an older woman slumped in her wheelchair positioned as close to the doors as possible. When the doors finally opened, employees and more able-bodied individuals helped push the ones in wheelchairs into the dining room. Joe even helped a woman in a wheelchair cross over the threshold into the open room.

Everyone had their assigned seat and Joe and I made our way to his designated table. There was an older man already sitting down waiting to be served. Joe made a brief introduction but it was clear he wanted to be left alone. As I gazed around the room, I noticed only one table where there were several couples sitting together. All the other tables were made up of only women or only men.

Once we sat down, a cheerful woman came over and served us baked chicken with just the right seasoning, potato salad, cooked spinach, and a home-baked roll. As Joe began to eat, I noticed he was having difficulty with chewing the chicken. As he realized the problem, he pushed his chair back and stated, "I forgot my teeth back in the room."

"I will be glad to go get them for you," I offered.

"No, I will be right back."

He pulled back from the table and slowly walked out the door. While Joe was gone, another man in a wheelchair joined us.

"Hello, my name is Andy."

"Hello, my name is Cora and I am here visiting Joe."

As we sat there, both feeling a little awkward, I decided to keep up the small talk. "Andy, where are you from?"

It was then I knew I had crossed the line from knowledge to confusion as a puzzled look swept across his face. It was clear he wanted to tell me but he just couldn't remember.

At that point, I could hear Joe's shuffling footsteps draw closer to the table. The walk to his room and back had clearly tired him out and he had to sit for a couple of minutes before finishing his lunch. After putting the last morsel of food in his mouth, he regarded me with a perplexed expression and asked, "Who did you come to visit?"

"Joe, I came to visit you."

"Don't you have some family near here that you are visiting?"

"No, Joe, I am here to just visit you."

He seemed satisfied with this response and took a sip from the milkshake that he received at each meal for extra calories.

I could tell that Joe had slipped into his own thoughts and decided to take advantage of this time to wonder about all the different people who had made this place home. From glancing around, I noticed people from several different ethnic and racial backgrounds. Everyone was definitely in their seventies or older.

But it wasn't the obvious that caught my attention but what lay beneath the surface. For starters, most everyone seemed content just eating. Very few even made an attempt at conversations. Only the couples seemed to be having quiet discussions.

Even though little was being said, lines had definitely been drawn and people understood their place. For instance, the man sitting at the table with Joe clearly didn't want to talk with someone of a different race but was eager to chat with the server or another man of his own race. On the other hand, I was very impressed with how the servers were attuned to the temperament of the residents and provided the necessary attention to make them happy.

Then, as if he knew I was ready to leave, Joe looked at me and asked, "What would you like to do now?"

"Let's go outside and sit in the sun."

We made our way out to the porch, past several Valentine arrangements and cheery window treatments. We found two rocking chairs and positioned them in the sun. At first we seemed content to just sit and soak in the warm rays on our faces. But then out of the blue, Joe asked, "What is that building on the other side of the parking lot?"

I looked in the direction he pointed to but saw nothing but trees. Instead of responding, I just sat, hoping that he would move on in his thoughts.

"How did I get here?" Joe asked.

"We brought you here. Don't you remember riding here with Mary Beth and Jay bringing your belongings in his truck?"

"Oh. Do you think if I get better I can go home?"

Hoping this conversation would be quickly forgotten I stated, "We will see, Joe. We'll see."

Chapter 53

*Trust in the Lord and do good; dwell in the land
and enjoy safe pasture.*
- Psalm 37:3

Valentine's Day at the Village was full of fun, good food, and catastrophes. Mary Beth arrived around 4:30 to join Joe in the dining room for the festivities. When she entered Joe's room, she was disturbed that he was still in the bed. "What are you doing here?"

"I'm here to take you to the Valentine's party in the dining room."

"Okay, let me get up and dressed." Joe slowly rolled over and pushed his body into a sitting position.

Mary Beth looked around the room and saw no sign of breakfast or lunch. "What did you eat for lunch today?"

"Nobody has brought me anything all day."

Instead of arguing with him, she moved into the other room to give him space to change his clothes. Once he had his pants and shirt on, she pulled out a dark red sweater for him to wear.

"Let's go down to the nurses' station before dinner. I brought some goody bags for them."

Joe seemed weaker than he had been recently and she convinced him that he should use the walker for the trip down the hall. Once they entered the hallway, other residents greeted them and told Joe how good it was to see him. This seemed to cheer him up and put some pep in his step.

The nurses seemed genuinely grateful for the goody bags and Joe was eager to take full credit for the treats. Mary Beth was just happy to see his mood brighten as they slowly made their way to the dining room.

Before they got to the door, music could be heard blaring out into the corridor. Joe shuffled up to his table and sat down in his usual chair. Mary Beth grabbed a chair and sat down next to her father. The music was a little too loud for Joe's liking, but it was clear that he was enjoying the festive atmosphere.

Both of them were looking toward the door when a woman came rushing through pushing her walker in full force. Before anyone could tell her about the cord that lay on the floor, her walker wheels caught the edge of the cord and she fell face down onto the floor. Immediately, blood started seeping from her head and she was clearly unconscious. A nurse assistant and a couple of other employees ran to her aid. Someone yelled to call an ambulance. After a few minutes, the woman began to stir and she was moved to the lobby. Someone came over with a wet cloth and cleaned the floor.

The music continued to play as Joe began to eat his dinner. After finishing most of his meal, he told Mary Beth that he wanted to go back to his room. It was obvious that he was exhausted from the event and wanted to rest.

Mary Beth called us on the way home to tell us about the evening. She shared that Joe had mentioned that the cancer must have moved from his neck to his lungs because he was having difficulty breathing. He told her that he remembered Jay taking him to a doctor but couldn't understand why no one had done anything to treat it.

Chapter 54

And if you do good to those who are good to you,
what credit is that to you?
- Luke 6:33

There is close to two inches of snow on the ground. Sounds like fun and it should have been except the weather forecasters didn't call for this snow. I went out this morning for a couple of items and got caught in the mini-blizzard. As I made my way home, I could tell that I was tensing up. So I slowed the car down to a crawl. Someone with a New York license plate sped past me. Probably thinking I shouldn't have been on the road, and he was probably right.

Many times during this last year, I have felt like we have been on a road that I shouldn't be on. The road has been treacherous in spots and I have intentionally tried to slow things down to a crawl so I can stay in control. But I'm not. If I have learned anything from this last year, it is that I am not in control. God is.

Recently, with Joe's health becoming stable and the house in Columbia on the verge of being sold, we seem to be drawing close to the end of our journey. But I am still haunted by the lack of resolution between Jay and Joe. Oh, I have wanted there to be a bond formed that could last for eternity. I have dreamed of a day where they truly embrace and allow forgiveness to replace the bitterness and anger that has been there for so long.

But the more I read about dementia, I am having a hard time believing that this can occur. It is like Joe's mind is stuck in a place that just can't go forward. His anger toward Jay has been cemented to his heart.

Two weeks ago, when Jay and I were leaving, I looked back after saying goodbye and saw Jay reach out to his father to give him a hug. An attempt to demonstrate his feelings toward this man that has caused him so much pain. But all I saw was an awkward embrace.

Guilt is a strong force that changes who we are. It can lay dormant in a conscious or subconscious state for a lifetime. But eventually, it comes out in one form or another. For Joe, the guilt from his treatment of his son has come forth like an erupting volcano. Even though he doesn't realize it, this emotion has taken the form of anger and a tendency to erase Jay's existence.

If it was just about the hug, I could probably move on but it is more. It is like Joe has pushed Jay out of his consciousness. Jay and I have driven to New Bern almost every week since Joe has been there. But when someone asks him if he has seen his son, he always says no. But if Joe becomes agitated, he always calls Jay to come fix the situation. It has almost become humorous when we see his name come up on caller ID. We will never forget when Joe called and started yelling at Jay to bring him some food. That no one was feeding him and that it was Jay's fault that he was out in the woods. Or the time that Joe had left the faucet on and flooded his room. Joe called demanding Jay come and take away the blowers used for drying the carpet.

On the other hand, I have realized once again why I fell in

love with my husband. Jay has demonstrated an unconditional love for his father and a loyalty toward his family that touches my heart to the core. Many times throughout this year, he has experienced depression, anger, and confusion but never once did he turn his back and walk away. He has grown as a brother, a father, a husband, but mostly as a son.

Joe continues to maintain his ability to get up and walk the distance to the front porch where he can be seen most days sitting in the sun and greeting the people that walk by. His dementia continues to impair his ability to remember our visits and all of the newfound memories that have been created over the last year. Even so, we have been able to tuck away the recollections of our time with him and are ever grateful for each and every one.

About the Author

Cora Darrah is a first time author. She has been married for thirty-six years and is the mother of two beautiful daughters. She is also a grandmother, and the daughter-in-law to Joe. Cora was a special educator for over thirty years. She specifically worked with children with intellectual disabilities and has a real passion for working with children that display autistic tendencies. Since retirement, she has been busy taking care of her three grandchildren, playing club tennis, and enjoying her two French Bulldogs. Whenever possible, you can find her and her husband Jay camping at a local state park with their dogs and grandchildren.

Cora has recently begun blogging about her personal spiritual walk with God. Each post focuses on how God works in all situations, even times of suffering. You can locate her latest blog at www.coradarrah.com.

Cora was inspired to write *Here We Go Joe* after spending the last eighteen months assisting her husband and sister-in-law with the emotional decision of moving Joe from his home in South Carolina to an assisted living community in North Carolina. Cora truly hopes this story of her own experience with Joe can assist and inspire other families going through the devastating effects of dementia.

Made in the USA
Charleston, SC
24 October 2015